MW01094324

The Wisdom of Richard Hooker

Selections from Hooker's Writings
with Topical Index

Philip B. Secor and Lee W. Gibbs

authorHOUSE™

1663 LIBERTY DRIVE, SUITE 200
BLOOMINGTON, INDIANA 47403
(800) 839-8640
WWW.AUTHORHOUSE.COM

© 2005 Philip B. Secor and Lee W. Gibbs. All Rights Reserved.

No part of this book may be reproduced, stored in a retrieval system, or transmitted by any means without the written permission of the author.

First published by AuthorHouse 07/11/05

ISBN: 1-4208-4818-6 (sc)

Library of Congress Control Number: 2005903218

Printed in the United States of America
Bloomington, Indiana

This book is printed on acid-free paper.

Topical Index

Preface

We are two Anglican churchmen united in this book by a single passion: to bring the wisdom of Richard Hooker, the founding theologian of the Anglican religious tradition, before the attention of the clergy and laity of Anglican and Episcopal churches throughout the world in a form that will make his helpful and healing insights widely available in our troubled and fractured age. The need is especially acute as Anglicans, in the face of schism, are looking back to their intellectual roots and to the primary apologist of their branch of the Church.

One of us is a priest and scholar in the Episcopal Church who is one of the editors of the authoritative *Folger Library Edition of the Works of Richard Hooker* (1974-1995) as well as the author of many scholarly articles and more popular tracts on Hooker's theology.[1] The other of

---

[1] Lee W. Gibbs, "Introduction and Commentaries on Books I and VI of Richard Hooker's, Of the Laws of Ecclesiastical Polity, vol. 6 of The Folger Library Edition of the Works of Richard Hooker, Medieval & Renaissance Texts and Studies, 1993, pp. 81-124, 249-308, 497-521, 833-94; "Richard Hooker," Sixteenth Century British Non-Dramatic Writers, First Series ed. by David H. Richardson in Dictionary of Literary Biography, Bruccoli Clark Layman, 1993, 130:192-209; The Middle Way: Voices of Anglicanism, Forward Movement, 1991; "Richard Hooker: Prophet of Anglicanism or English Magisterial Reformer?" Anglican Theological Review, 84 (2002), 943-60; "Richard Hooker's Via Media Doctrine of Scripture and Tradition, Harvard Theological Review, vol. 95, No. 2 (2002), pp.227-35; "Theology, Logic and Rhetoric in the Temple Controversy Between Richard Hooker and Walter Travers," Anglican Theological Review, 65 (1983), 177-88.

us is a life-long church layman who is the author of the only full biography of Hooker, first published in 1999, and of two modern editions of large segments of Hooker's writings that present some of his most important ideas in contemporary English.[2] Both of us have preached, written, and lectured for many years, inside the Church and without, in order to bring Hooker's wisdom to as wide an audience as possible.

In this volume we have joined forces to offer what we think are the most compelling and helpful of Hooker's insights in a form that we hope will make them readily available to seminarians trying to make sense of Hooker's sometimes beautiful but often arcane prose, ministers preparing sermons, laypeople in their devotional readings, and anyone seeking some help in leading their lives in our troubled times. The selections we have chosen are arranged alphabetically by topic. An easy to use index is provided so that subjects of interest can be found quickly. In a few instances we have repeated selections that seemed to belong under more than one heading.

We have "translated" Hooker's often-difficult prose into modern English, taking care not to distort his meaning or rob his dynamic style of its vigour. In most instances, the changes are made only to modernize grammar, spelling, and punctuation, and to make some of Hooker's long sentences more succinct. Since the book is not intended for professional theologians or

---

[2]Philip B. Secor, <u>Richard Hooker, Prophet of Anglicanism</u>, Burns & Oates/Anglican Book Centre, 1999, Continuum Books, 2001; <u>The Sermons of Richard Hooker, A Modern Edition</u>, SPCK, 2001; <u>Richard Hooker on Anglican Faith and Worship: Of the Laws of Ecclesiastical Polity, Book V: A Modern Edition</u>, SPCK, 2003.

other scholars, we have not given page references for our selections. We have, however, provided book and chapter references for those who wish to read further in either the *Folger Edition* or Secor's modern editions of the sermons and Book V of the *Laws*.

Hooker, of course, was a man of his times and not ours. We have not attempted to sanitize his ideas to make them more compatible with modern sensibilities. When he discusses such issues as clergy qualifications--which he thought often needed to be kept low in order to have at least warm bodies in the sanctuary--or preaching, which he was inclined to denigrate because he felt the Calvinist extremists of his day placed far too much emphasis on that part of the worship service--he was addressing issues specific to his time. Although his view of women was surprisingly enlightened for his day, many will find him condescending or even offensive. One of the few allowances we have made for modern convention is to render Hooker's use of the male pronoun non gender-specific whenever that does not alter his meaning or make a garble of his sentences.

For readers not familiar with Hooker, this much may suffice as an introduction. He was born in 1554 in the village of Heavitree, just outside the walls of the city of Exeter in western England. This was the year when Mary Tudor, known to history as "Bloody Mary", became Queen, re-established Roman Catholicism in Protestant England and unleashed terrible persecution of reformed clergy--about as horrendous as that committed against Roman Catholics several years earlier by her half-brother, Edward VI. A member of the poor branch of a prominent Exeter family, young Hooker was a bright lad, did well in grammar school, went to Oxford under the patronage of John Jewel, Bishop of Salisbury and the first major apologist of the Church of England. At Oxford he earned his bachelor's and masters degrees, was ordained a priest in the Church, and soon became a renowned professor and scholar, teacher of the sons of some of the most famous men in England. The new Queen, Elizabeth I, learned that Hooker was teaching and preaching a more tolerant brand of faith and worship that was congenial with her own desire to establish a broad church in which Protestants and Catholics alike could worship without recourse to the hatred and killing in the name of religion that had characterized English life since the death of her father, Henry VIII.

In 1584 Queen Elizabeth brought the thirty-year old Hooker down from Oxford and made him Master (Rector) of the prestigious Temple Church in London where many of the judges, lawyers, and other influential men of the day worshipped each Sunday. For six years Hooker preached what he later expanded and refined in his great book, *Of the Laws of Ecclesiastical Polity*, and what later still became the foundation of Anglicanism. In his writings he also expressed some of the most eloquent definitions of law in western literature and was one of the first to develop modern ideas of constitutional government and popular sovereignty, extending and refining the medieval political theories of Bracton and Fortescue and influencing the later ideas of Locke, Jefferson and Madison. He has also been long regarded as an exemplar of Elizabethan prose writing and is claimed as a champion as often by devotees and scholars of English literature as he is by political theorists and theologians.

We offer our thanks to the publishers, editors and commentators of *The Folger Library Edition of the Works of Richard Hooker.* Without this monumental edition of Hooker's writings there would not have been an authoritative text on which to base this work and Philip Secor's earlier modern editions of Hooker's sermons and Book V of the *Polity.* Lee Gibbs would like to acknowledge the kind invitation of Philip Secor to participate in this joint venture, and to thank his wife, Joan, for her enthusiastic support from the very beginning of this project. Philip Secor thanks his wife, Anne, for similar encouragement and also expresses thanks to Annette Kirk, President of the Russell Kirk Center for Cultural Renewal for providing the congenial intellectual retreat within which this work was begun. Both editors express the hope that this book will make the wisdom of Richard Hooker available and accessible to a wider audience than ever before.

Philip B. Secor   November 2, 2004
Lee W. Gibbs

The Wisdom of Richard Hooker

Absolution (See Also Confession)

Sin is relieved only by the assurance of pardon. Therefore, it remains for us to consider what hope we have for forgiveness when the action of a mere human being supposedly absolves us from sin committed against God. (VI,6)

Our Savior, when he spoke the words, "those whose sins you remit are remitted" (John 20:23), ordained judges over sinful souls. He gave them authority to absolve from sin and promised to ratify in heaven whatever they did on earth in execution of their office. He did this so that His ministers might be encouraged to do their duty with all faithfulness, and so that His people might be admonished with all reverence to be governed by them. In this way, both know the function of the one towards the other and know that this way assures us of the promise of His perpetual assistance and approval. (VI,6)

Ministerial absolution has two effects. With regard to sin, it only declares us free from the guilt thereof and that we are restored to God's favor. But concerning our right to participate in sacred and divine mysteries, of which through sin we were made unworthy, the Church, upon our apparent repentance, truly restores our liberty, looses the chains that had tied us, remits all that is past, and accepts us as no less returned than as if we had never gone astray. (VI,6)

The ministerial sentence of private absolution is no more than a declaration of what God has done. (VI,8)

—— *Angels* ——

Let us now lift up our eyes, as it were, from the footstool to the throne of God and consider the state of heavenly and divine creatures. Angels are immaterial and intellectual creatures, the glorious inhabitants of those sacred palaces, where there is nothing but light and blessed immortality with no shadow of tears, discontent, grief, and uncomfortable passions but only joy, tranquility, and peace for ever and ever. They are in number and order huge, mighty, and royal armies. They stand in perfect obedience to that law which the Highest (whom they adore, love and imitate) has imposed upon them. (I,4)

God, who moves mere natural creatures only in a causative manner, moves intellectual creatures differently-- especially His holy angels. Beholding the face of God, they all adore Him in admiration of so great an excellency. Rapt with the love of His beauty, they cleave inseparably unto Him for ever. Desire to resemble Him in goodness makes them tireless and even insatiable in their longing to do by all means all manner of good unto all the creatures of God--but especially unto the children of human beings. (I,4)

Angelic actions may be reduced to these three general kinds: first, most delectable love arising from the visible apprehension of the purity, glory, and beauty of God, which are invisible to all except to spirits who are pure; secondly, adoration grounded upon the evidence of the greatness of God, upon whom they see that all things depend; thirdly, imitation bred by the presence of His exemplary goodness, Who does not cease, in their sight, daily to fill heaven and earth with the rich treasures of His most free and undeserved grace. (I,4)

Angels are linked into a kind of corporation among themselves, and also with humans. Consider angels each one separately and their law is that which the Prophet David mentions: "All you angels praise Him" (Psalm 148:2). Consider the angels of God in association with one another, and their law is that which arranges them as an army, one in order and degree above another. Finally, consider the angels as having with us humans that communion which the Apostle to the Hebrews notes (Hebrews 12:22) and, in this regard, angels have not disdained to profess themselves our fellow servants. (I,4)

— *Apocrypha* —

Everyone knows that we do not regard the Apocrypha as sacred--as we do Holy Scripture--but rather see these books as human creations dealing with divine matters. (V,20)

If in what we read there happens to be a clause, a sentence, or even a whole speech that seems to have some error in it, should the mixture of a little dross constrain the Church from gaining so much gold--all for the sake of maintaining a strict separation between Scripture and these books of the Apocrypha? (V,20)

We should not lump all the residue of writings apart from Scripture haphazardly into one pile and abolish them all. It is not incongruous to discard the false legends about the martyrs and yet retain homilies and the old Ecclesiastical Books of the Apocrypha. If I thought, as some do, that it was safer and wiser not to read these Books in public, I would, nevertheless--in this and similar matters--be reluctant to oppose my private judgment in the face of reverend church authority. (V,20)

— *Apostasy* —

That which separates anyone utterly, that which cuts him off cleanly from the visible Church is simple apostasy--a direct denial and complete rejection of the entire Christian faith. (V,68)

— *Apostolic Succession* —

The first bishops in the Church of Christ were his blessed Apostles... . Those who were called Apostles, because they were sent by Christ to publish His Gospel throughout the world, were also called bishops because the care of government was committed to them in such a way that they performed the offices of their episcopal authority by governing even as they performed their apostolic authority by teaching. (VII,4)

The Apostles were sent as specially chosen eyewitnesses of Jesus Christ, from whom they immediately received their complete appointment and commission to be the first founders of a House of God consisting of Gentiles and Jews. In this commission there are no others like them.

And yet the Apostles now have their successors, if not in scope and importance surely in the general character of their episcopal function, whereby they have power to sit as spiritual judges over both laity and clergy wherever Christian churches have been established. (VII,4)

Whether bishops admit people to the fellowship of saints or exclude them from it, whether they bind offenders or set them again at liberty, whether they remit or retain sins--whatsoever is done by way of orderly and lawful proceeding, the Lord Himself has promised to ratify. This is that grand original warrant (Matthew 18:18; John 20:23) by force of which the guides and prelates in God's Church, first His Apostles (1 Timothy 1:20), and afterwards others following them successively, both used and upheld that discipline, the end of which is to heal the consciences of humans, to cure their sins, to reclaim offenders from iniquity, and to make them just by repentance. (VI,4)

—— *Apostles* ——

Has not God chosen the refuse of the world, the outcasts of society, to be the light of the world? What of the very Apostles of Christ? Here are men unlearned, yet how filled with understanding; few in number, yet how great in power; contemptible in appearance, yet how clothed in the Spirit. How wonderful they are! (First Sermon on Jude).

If I wish to gain true understanding, whom shall I seek to teach me? Shall I get me to the schools of the Greeks? Why? These men of worldly wisdom are ignorant because they have rejected the wisdom of God. Shall I beseech the scribes and interpreters of the law to be my teachers? How can they be wise when they are offended by the cross of Christ? I must have a true teacher because it is death for me to be ignorant of the great mystery of the Son of God. Yet I would have been ignorant forever were it not for one of the Apostles of Jesus, a poor fisherman, unknown, unlearned, recently emerging from a boat with clothes wringing wet, who opened his inspired mouth and taught me. These Apostles, these poor simple folk, have made us rich in the knowledge of the mysteries of Christ. (First Sermon on Jude)

Concerning the Apostles, He who gave them from above such miraculous powers to confirm what they taught also endued them with wisdom to teach that which those miracles confirmed. Our Savior chose twelve simple and unlearned men, so that the greater their lack of wisdom, the more admirable might appear that which God supernaturally endued them with from heaven. Persons, therefore, who knew the poor and miserable estate in which these men had lived, could not help but marvel when they heard the wisdom of their speech, and therefore, were so much more attentive to their teaching. For they studied no particular language; rather, they spoke with all. Of themselves, they were uneducated and did not know even how to deliberate; the Spirit gave them speech and eloquent utterance. (III,8)

Our Lord and Savior in Matthew's Gospel (Matthew 16:19) gave His Apostles general rule over God's Church. For they who have the keys of the kingdom of heaven are thereby signified to be stewards of the House of God. Under God, they guide, command, judge and correct His Family. (VI,4)

The Apostles' office consists in different functions, some belonging to doctrine, some to discipline--all contained in the name "keys." Therefore, they have for matters of discipline, both litigious and criminal, their courts and consistories erected by the heavenly authority of His most sacred voice, who said, "Tell the Church" (Matthew 18:17). They are armed with the power to eject out of the Church those rebellious and stubborn persons who refuse to obey their sentence; to deprive them of the honors, rights and privileges of Christian people; to treat them as if they were heathen and publicans hated by society. (VI,4)

— *Archbishops* —

Even from early times, there has always been one kind of bishop who is superior only over presbyters, and another kind who also have preeminence over other bishops. We here consider in what respect inequality of bishops was thought at first to be something that would be expedient for the Church. We will look at the difference between them, focusing upon how much the power of one has been larger, higher, and greater than that of the other. The reasons why it was thought appropriate that bishops not be equal in every way are the same reasons both in the wisdom of God and of human beings. Such wisdom dictates that it is most necessary, when many governors must of necessity concur for the ordering of the same affairs, for one individual to have some kind of sway or power that is greater than the rest. For where there are a number of persons, there must be order; otherwise, there will be confusion. (VII,8)

The great Council of Nicaea, which was held only three hundred twenty four years after our Savior Christ, declared, even then, that certain metropolitans had historic pre-eminence and dignity above the others, namely, the primates of Alexandria, Rome, and Antioch. (VII,8)

—— *Atheism* ——

Those who see no God at all are few in number and, for the vulgarity of their minds, hardly deserve the name of human beings. We should judge those people to be the most miserable of all creatures were it not for an even more wretched sort, the atheists, whom nature has disposed to go about saying that God is no God. The fountain and wellspring of this impiety is a determination to reap whatever sensual profits or pleasures the world can provide and not be prevented from using any means available to get them. I think no one will doubt that this is the real cause of atheism when he considers what pains atheists take to destroy major incentives and motivations to live virtuously, namely: God's creation of the world, the care of God for His creation, the resurrection of the dead, the joys of heaven and the endless pains of the wicked, and, above all else, the authority of Scripture. On these items atheists continuously hammer, as well as on the immortality of the soul, which follows from all the rest. (V,2)

— *Atonement ("Satisfaction")* —

The word "satisfaction", as the ancient Fathers used it, contained whatever a penitent should do to humble himself before God, and to bear witness by those deeds of contrition that were promised in his confession... . Satisfaction is a work that justice requires be done for the contentment of persons who have been injured. It is not a sufficient satisfaction in the eye of justice unless it is fully equal to the injury for which satisfaction is being made. Seeing that the sin against God is eternal and infinite, it is necessarily an infinite wrong. Justice in this regard must, therefore, exact an infinite recompense or else inflict upon the offender an infinite punishment. Since God has thus to be satisfied and human beings are not able to make such satisfaction, He, out of His unspeakable love and inclination to save humankind from eternal death, ordained on our behalf a Mediator to do that which for any other would have been impossible. Wherefore, all sin is remitted by faith alone in Christ's passion, and no one is justified without such belief. Christ's satisfaction is ours by that faith alone which, after sin, makes us His by conversion. (VI,5)

Our Lord Jesus Christ, by His one most precious and propitiatory sacrifice, which was His body--a gift of infinite worth offered for the sins of the whole world-- has thereby once for all reconciled us to God, purchased God's general and free pardon, and turned away divine indignation from humankind. (VI,5)

The most respected among the works of satisfaction have always been these three: prayers, fasts, and almsgiving. (VI,5)

— Baptism —

We rightly declare Baptism to be the door of our entrance into God's house, the first apparent beginning of our new life, the sign, perhaps, of the grace of our earlier election, and the first step in our sanctification. (V,60)

Family

Baptism is an action that is partly moral, partly ecclesiastical, and partly mystical. It is moral in that it is a duty that people perform before God. It is ecclesiastical in that it is the duty of God's Church to offer it. Finally, it is mystical to the extent that we believe in what God intends to perform by means of it. (V,62)

Baptism is a sacrament that God has instituted in His Church so that those who receive it might be incorporated into Christ and thus, by His precious merit, obtain by imputation, that saving grace that takes away all former guilt. By this sacrament we are also infused with the divine virtue of the Holy Ghost that gives to the soul its first disposition toward newness of life. (V,60)

Later in life, when we acknowledge that which we professed as children without any understanding, are we doing anything else but bringing to ripeness the seed that was sown in Baptism? We are at that earlier time believers because we are beginning a process that time will perfect. Until we come to actual full faith, the sacrament is a shield as strong as faith itself against all opposing infernal powers. (V,64)

The outward expressions of the mystical perfection of Baptism are the element of water, the Holy Word, and the proper application of both by the minister to the person receiving the sacrament. If we add to these the hidden reference in the sacrament to new life and remission of sins by virtue of Christ's covenant with His

Church, there is nothing more required to accomplish fully the sacrament of Baptism. (V,62)

Baptism is far more important than any rite or solemnity that may be devised to administer it. (V,58)

In case of necessity where there can be no delay, Baptism may properly be administered without the usual rites and solemnities, rather than to allow anyone to depart this life without the sacrament. (V,58)

The letter of Scripture clearly and expressly requires two things as necessary for Baptism: *water* and *Spirit*. Water is the duty required of us; Spirit is a gift that God bestows. There is danger in presuming to interpret this as if the clause that concerns our part is unnecessary. (V,59)

If Christ Himself, who gave us salvation, had to be baptized, it is not for us who seek salvation to annoy and press Him as to whether un-baptized people may be saved. (V,60)

Although God might, in the hidden ways of His incomprehensible mercy, be thought to save some persons without Baptism, that does not relieve the Church from responsibility if, through her excessive scrupulousness, requirements, and unimportant impediments, she should cause so important a grace to be withheld from anyone. (V,60)

Since grace is not absolutely tied to the sacrament of Baptism, God is lenient in not binding us to what is impossible for us. He accepts our good intention for the deed itself when we cannot do what we should. Since there is a presumed desire and intention on the part of parents and the Church that Baptism should be given to infants, a remorseful sense of equity has moved a number of church scholars ingeniously to grant that an all-merciful God imparts a hidden desire for Baptism to others on behalf of infants. God accepts this desire as if it came from the infants themselves rather than cast away their souls for something that could not be helped. (V,60)

The reasons that apply to prohibiting women from baptizing in a church service are no justifiable bar to and do not negate the practices of those churches that allow private Baptisms to be administered by women under extreme conditions. (V,62)

The grace of Baptism comes as a gift from God. God committed the ministry of Baptism to special men only for the sake of order in His Church and not because the authority of those men would add force to the sacrament itself. (V,62)

Just as no defect in the calling of those who teach the truth can take away the benefit to those who hear it, so the lack of lawful calling in those who baptize cannot make their baptisms without effect for those who receive them. (V,62)

There is a false notion among some ministers that no infant may receive the sacrament of Baptism unless at least one of the parents is known by soundness of faith and virtuous living to be a child of God. This idea has led some ministers to reject children if the parents are mistaken in their religious beliefs or have been excommunicated for some other reason. Others would withhold Baptism unless the father, even if no exception is taken to his beliefs, makes a profession of his faith and swears that the child is his. Where God has made these men ministers of holy things, they make themselves inquisitors of people's personal lives much more than is necessary. They should remember that God ordained Baptism as a gift to mankind. To withhold this gift is odious. To expand it is acceptable both to God and man. (V,64)

As Christ has died and risen from the dead but once, so the sacrament that, through Him, extinguishes sin and begins new life in us, can be available only once in our lives and by only one administration of it. A second Baptism has always been abhorred in God's Church as a kind of incestuous birth. (V,62)

—— *Bishops* ——

Bishops have always been in existence as long as the Church has been in existence. The Apostles themselves who planted the Church ruled as bishops over it. They could not have kept things so well in order during their own times had they not had that episcopal authority which was given to them from above--an authority which they exercised far and wide over all other guides and pastors of God's Church. (VII,13)

The Apostles of our Lord, in accord with those directions that were given to them from above, erected churches in all those cities that received the Word of truth, the Gospel of God. All the churches that were erected by them received the same faith, the same sacraments, the same form of governance. The form of government that was first established by them was a college of ecclesiastical persons who were appointed in every city for that purpose. In their writings, they sometimes call these persons presbyters, and at other times bishops. (VII,5)

Therefore, let us not fear to be bold and preemptory in stating that, if there were anything in the Church's government which was first instituted, it certainly had to be the institution of bishops; for the institution of bishops was from heaven, even from God; the Holy Spirit was the author of it. (VII,5)

This we boldly set down as a most infallible truth: that the Church of Christ is at this day lawfully (and has been so since the beginning) governed by bishops who have permanent superiority and ruling power over other ministers of the Word and sacraments. (VII,3)

For a thousand five hundred years and more, the Church of Christ has continued under the sacred rule of bishops. During this time, Christianity has never been planted in any kingdom throughout the world without this kind of government, a government that I am resolutely persuaded has been ordained by God as much as any other kind of government in the world is of God. In this realm of England, before the Normans, yea even before the Saxons, there were Christians whose chief pastors of their souls were bishops. This order of ministry continued from about the time of the first establishment of Christian religion (which was publicly begun through the virtuous disposition of King Lucius not fully two hundred years after Christ) continued until the coming of the Saxons. The Saxons replanted paganism everywhere, except for one part of the Island where the ancient natural inhabitants, the Britains, were driven. The Britains retained constantly the faith of Christ, together with the same form of spiritual rule that their fathers before them had received. Therefore, in the histories of the Church we find very ancient mention made of our own bishops. (VII,1)

Among ecclesiastical persons bishops are the most important. A bishop's function must be defined by that in which his superiority consists. A bishop is a minister of God, to whom there is given permanent power to administer the Word and Sacraments. This is a power other presbyters have but a bishop also has the further power to ordain ecclesiastical persons, as well as the power of primary authority over presbyters and the laity as well--a power to be a pastor to pastors themselves. So that the individual in this office, since he is a presbyter or a pastor, shares those things that are common to him and other pastors: the ministering of the Word and sacraments. But those things pertaining to his office that properly make him a bishop cannot be shared with other pastors. (VII,2)

The name "bishop" has been borrowed from the Greeks, for whom it signifies one who has principal charge in guiding and overseeing others. The same word in ecclesiastical writings is applied to church governors, at first to all and not just to the chief among them; in a short time, however, the term came to signify only that episcopal authority which the principal governors exercised over the rest. (VII,2)

In a bishop there are three things to be considered: the power whereby he is distinguished from other pastors, the special portion of the clergy and people over whom he is to exercise that episcopal power, and the place of his seat or throne together with the profits, preeminence, and honors attached to it. (VIII,7)

And as is the case with pastors, so likewise it is with bishops who, being principal pastors, are so either at large or else "with restraint." They are at large when the subject of their authority is indefinite and not tied to any certain place. Bishops are "with restraint" when their governance in the Church is contained within some definite local boundary, beyond which their jurisdiction does not reach. This is what we always mean when we speak of that regiment by bishops which we hold to be most lawful, divine, and holy in the Church of Christ. (VII,2)

— *Calvin, John* —

The new [Presbyterian] discipline had a founder whom I think from my own perspective to be from the hour he appeared incomparably the wisest man who was ever enjoyed by the French Church. He was educated in the civil law. He gathered divine knowledge not so much from hearing or reading as by teaching others. Though thousands were indebted to him for that kind of knowledge, his only guide was God, the author of that most blessed fountain, the Book of Life, along with his own remarkable dexterity of wit and the help of other learning. Having been forced to leave France, he fell at length upon Geneva. (Preface,2)

What the Master of the *Sentences* [Peter Lombard] was in the Church of Rome, the same and more is Calvin among the preachers of reformed churches. The most perfect divines are judged to be those who are most skillful in Calvin's writings. His books are almost the very canon used to judge both doctrine and discipline. French churches, both abroad and at home in their own country, are all cast in the mold that Calvin made. The Church of Scotland, in erecting the form of its reformation, took the self-same pattern. (Preface,2)

—— *Ceremonies* ——

Ceremonies carry more weight than is apparent to the eye. They work because of long, common usage, even though in their particular acts we hardly see what they are good for. Because their usefulness is not, for the most part, clearly understood, superstition is apt to impute to them greater value than they actually have. (V,65)

What rite or custom is there that is so harmless that the wit of man could not bend itself to derision and easily find something to scorn and make jest of? (V,73)

The best course for those who would remedy the superstitious abuses and practices in the Church that are otherwise valuable is not to abolish their use altogether simply because they think that not using them at all is the remedy for wrongly using them. Rather they should try to bring them back to a proper and perfect religious use. (V,65)

—— *Choice* ——

To choose is to will one thing over another. To will is to bend our souls to the having or doing of that which we see to be good. Goodness is seen with the eye of understanding, and the light of that eye is reason. So there are two principle fountains of human action:

knowledge and will. The will tending toward any end is called choice. (I,7)

— *Chosen People (The Elect)* —

When God created Adam, He created us. We who are descended from Adam have within us the root from which we have sprung. However, we are not the children of God except by His special grace and favor. The children of God are the race and progeny of His own natural Son, who is a second Adam who came from heaven. They are His children by spiritual and heavenly birth. These chosen people were in God as savior and not only as creator. The grace of God's *saving* goodness, *saving* wisdom, and *saving* power inclined itself toward them. Those who were in God eternally, because they were chosen to have new life, have God within them either by His adoption or His calling, just as the artificer is in the work that is formed by his hand. (V,56)

— *Christ (Christology)* —

There are only **four ingredients** that combine to make up the whole of our Lord Jesus Christ: His divinity, His manhood, the combination of these two, and the distinction that remained between the two when they were joined. There are **four major heresies** that have stood against these four truths: first, the Arians, by arguing against the divinity of Christ; secondly, the Apollinarians, by distorting and misinterpreting that which belongs to His human nature; thirdly, the Nestorians, by rending Christ asunder and dividing

Him into two persons; fourthly, the Eutychians, by confounding in His person the two natures that they should have distinguished. Against these four heresies there have been **four Councils** of the ancient Church: the Council of Nicea, to defend the Church from the Arians; the Council of Constantinople, against the Apollinarians; the Council of Ephesus, against the Nestorians; The Council of Chalcedon, against the Eutychians. (V,54)

Finally, in **four words** we may fully abridge all that the ancient Fathers and Councils have declared about Christian belief, either directly or in refuting heresies: they have spoken *truly, perfectly, indivisibly, and distinctly.* They have spoken *truly* when speaking of Christ as God; *perfectly*, when speaking of Christ's manhood, *indivisibly*, when speaking of Christ's being as having both natures, and *distinctly*, when speaking of Christ's continuing to be one person. (V,54)

There remains a singular unity of the three substances in the Father. The Son is in the Father as light is in that light which it creates and never leaves. In this respect, since Christ's eternal being comes from the Father, who is His very life, it may be said that Christ lives by and through the Father. Since everyone loves his offspring as himself and is more or less alive in them, Christ, as the sole offspring of God, is the most dearly beloved of God. (V,56)

The nature of God being unified, there are not separate wills in God even though the Godhead consists of several Persons. On the other hand, in Christ there are two wills because he has two natures: the nature of God and the nature of man, each of which implies the faculty and power of will. Otherwise, Christ would not be both God and man. On this issue the Church long ago condemned the Monothelites as heretics for holding that Christ had but one will. (V,48)

Some things Christ does as God because His deity alone is the wellspring from which they flow. Some things He does as man because they issue from His merely human nature. Some things he does as both man and God simultaneously because both of His natures concur therein. There is often cooperation between His two natures, always an association between them, but never any mutual participation through which the properties of one are infused into the other. (V,53)

A kind of mutual exchange occurs whereby, when we speak of Christ, the concrete names "God" and "man" become interchangeable so that, in a manner of speaking, it does not matter whether we say that the Son of God created the world and that the Son of man, by His death, saved it, or we say that the Son of man created and the Son of God saved the world. (V,53)

Whenever we attribute to God what belongs to the manhood of Christ or to Christ's manhood what is inherent in His divinity, we understand by the words "God" and "man" not one nature or the other but the whole Person of Christ within which both natures reside. (V,53)

That part of Christ that is His manhood is not omnipresent but tied to a particular place. Yet He is present everywhere, in some sense, by a kind of *conjunction* with the divine part of His Person. The manhood of Christ may thus be said to be omnipresent in the sense that the divine substance in His Person is never severed from His manhood. (V,55)

The substance of Christ's body has only a localized presence. His body was not seen everywhere, nor did it everywhere suffer death, nor was it entombed everywhere, nor is it now exalted everywhere for being in heaven. There is no greater proof that Christ had a real human body than the properties of that body itself, including its particularity and specific location. (V,55)

That which the Father does as Lord and King over all He does not without the Son but with Him. The Son, through coeternal generation, receives from the Father that power which the Father has of Himself. For this reason, our Savior's words concerning His own dominion are, "To me all power both in heaven and on earth is given." The Father, by the Son, created and guided all things. Therefore, Christ has supreme dominion over the whole universal world. Christ is God, Christ is λόγος, the consubstantial Word of God; Christ is also that consubstantial Word made man. As God He has said of himself: "I am Alpha and Omega, the beginning and the end; He who was, who is, and who is to come, even the very omnipotent" (Rev. 1:8). As the consubstantial Word of God, He had with God before the beginning of the world that glory which as man He requested to have: "Father, glorify your Son now with that glory which I enjoyed before the world was" (John. 17:5). There is no necessity that all things spoken about Christ should agree in referring to Him either as God or man; rather, sometimes He is referred to as the consubstantial Word of God, and sometimes as the Word incarnate. (VIII,4)

The works of supreme dominion which have been wrought from the very beginning by the power of the Son of God are now most truly and properly the works of the Son of Man. The Word made flesh sits forever and reigns as sovereign Lord over all. Dominion belongs to the kingly office of Christ. Propitiation and mediation belong to His priestly office. Instruction belongs to His pastoral and prophetic office. His works of dominion are in different degrees and kind according to the different conditions of those who are subject to His power. He presently governs and hereafter shall judge the world in its entirety. Therefore, His regal power cannot in truth be restricted to only a portion of the world. (VIII,4)

— *Christian Living (Ethics)* —

As people who, living out their natural lives, are nourished by nature, so the person to whom the Spirit of Christ gives life also delights in his spiritual food. He "hungers after righteousness." It is meat and drink for him to be engaged in doing good works. (Sermon on Pride)

Whenever malice would work evil and yet avoid the appearance of evil intent, the color with which it paints itself is always a fair and plausible pretense of seeking to further what is good. (V,32)

It cannot be endured to hear someone openly profess that he set his neighbor's house on fire but prayed that it would not burn. (V,29)

To do the same thing that Christ did in every comparable situation would be to follow in His footsteps in a way that would cause us to stray more from His purposes than we do by not following Him with such severe rigidity. (V,68)

When neither of two wrongs can be avoided, the choice of the lesser evil is not sinful. Wrongs, as I see it, should be judged to be inevitable when there is no apparent way to avoid them. (V,9)

The motions of people who live the life of God have a special excellence. Their hands are not stretched out toward their enemies except to give them alms. Their feet are slow except when they are traveling for the benefit of their brothers and sisters. When they are railed at by wicked persons, they reply with the words of Stephen, "Lord, lay not this thing to their charge." If we could live three times as long as Methuselah, or live as long as the moon will endure, what would our natural life amount to without this new life in Christ? This new life alters our corrupt nature. By this new life we are continually stirred up to do good things. We are led to abhor the gross defilements of this wicked world, yet constantly and patiently to suffer whatever befalls us as though "as sheep we are led by flocks to the slaughter." (Sermon on Pride)

We may set it down as a solid axiom that when we denigrate and transgress our duty to God, which by our very nature we are supposed to observe, we lose the benefits that the things of this world, each working according to its own nature, might otherwise have yielded to us. (Sermon on Proverbs/Matthew/Hebrews)

Whatever in nature excels in pre-eminence and honor is of greatest value and benefit to other things. This fact should be an inducement to God's children to delight in imparting to others the good that has been bestowed upon them in proportion to what they have received. The good things in life are known to be communicable by those who possess them; they are known to be derived from others and to be transferable to those in need of them. In these transactions lies the exercise of justice. (Sermon on Pride)

Which of you will willingly remain in a misshapen or broken down house? Knowing that we are the temples of the Holy Ghost, shall we then allow sin and vanity to drop into our eyes and ears and cover every corner of our bodies and souls? Which of you receives a guest whom he honors or loves and does not clean his chamber before the guest arrives? Shall we allow the chamber of our hearts and consciences to be full of vomit, full of filth, full of garbage, knowing that Christ has said, "I and my Father will come and dwell with you"? Is it proper for your oxen to lie in parlors and you to lodge in animal cribs? Is it seemly for you to dwell in your fine houses while the house of the Almighty lies in waste--the very house that you yourselves are? (Second Sermon on Jude)

The difference between right and crooked minds is in the means they follow and avoid in pursuit of their goals. (Sermon on Pride)

It may seem a paradox but it is true that no wicked person's condition is ever really prosperous, fortunate or happy. So what if they bless themselves and think themselves very happy? Do not demented persons often have a high opinion of their own wisdom? It may be that others think of them as they think of themselves. But what others are these? Surely people just like them. Truth and reason view such people differently. (Sermon on Remedy Against Sorrow and Fear)

There has crept into the minds of people in these days a secret, pernicious, and pestilent idea that the greatest perfection of a Christian consists in the discovery of other people's faults and in clever discourse about their own faith. When the world abounded with just and righteous people, their chief concern was the exercise of piety, in which, for their safest direction, they harkened reverently to the reading of the law of God and kept in mind the oracles and aphorisms of that wisdom that tended to lead to a virtuous life. In our day we are more confident, not because our knowledge or judgment are more mature but because our desires are different from theirs. Their scope was obedience; ours is skill. Their endeavor was reformation of life; our virtue is nothing more than to hear gladly the rebuke of vice. They wore out their knees and hands in the practice of religion; we wear out our ears and our tongues. (V,81)

We may say that God prefers adverbs to verbs because the purpose of His law in appointing what we must do is our own perfection. This perfection consists chiefly in a virtuous attitude that shows itself to God not by *doing* but by doing *well.* In this distinction lies the difference between human and divine laws, the first content with *opus operatum* (what we do) and the second requiring *opus operantis* (how we do it). The one involves the deed; the other primarily the attitude of mind. Thus, according to the laws that apply principally to the hearts of men, religious acts that are not religiously performed can never be perfect. (V,62)

There is no apparent absurdity in thinking that all humans endowed with the use of reason are generally either good or evil. Whatever is good is approved by God. Moreover, the kinds of divine approbation are multiplied according to different degrees of goodness. Some things are good, yet in such a minimum degree that people are allowed to do them but are not praised for such acts by God. Examples are: "No one hates his own flesh" (Ephesians 5:29); "If you do good to those who do so to you, the very publicans themselves do as much" (Matthew 5:46); "They who have no care to provide for their own are worse than infidels" (1 Timothy 5:8). In actions of this kind, the very light of nature alone may discover that which is allowable in the sight of God. (II,8)

— *The Church* —

The Church is, to us, the very mother of our new birth in whose womb we are all bred and at whose breasts we receive nourishment. (V,50)

The Church is in Christ as Eve was in Adam. Yes, by grace every one of us is in Christ and in His Church, even as by nature we are in our first parents. God made Eve out of the rib of Adam. He formed His Church out of the flesh, the wounded and bleeding side of the Son of man. (V,56)

That Church of Christ, which we properly term His mystical body, can be but one. But no one can actually see that one Church because some of its members are already in heaven with Christ. As for the rest who are here on earth, we cannot discern in what manner they are truly and infallibly of that body even though their natural persons are visible to us. Our minds are able only by intellectual conceptualization to apprehend that there is such a real body, a collective body because it contains a huge multitude and a mystical body because the mystery of their conjunction is removed altogether from sense. Whatever we read in Scripture concerning the endless love and the saving mercy that God shows towards His Church, the only proper subject thereof is this Church. It is concerning this flock that our Lord and Savior has promised, "I give them eternal life, and they shall never perish, neither shall any pluck them out of my hands. (John 10:28). (III,1)

Those who are of this society [the Church] have unique marks and signs that distinguish them from all others. But these people are clear and manifest only to God, who sees their hearts and understands and understands all their secret cogitations. (III,1)

The visible Church is but one, continued from the first beginning of the world to the last end. This company is divided into two sorts: the one before, the other since the coming of Christ. That part which since the coming of Christ has partly embraced and shall hereafter more fully embrace the Christian religion, we call more properly the Church of Christ. The Apostle [Paul] affirms plainly of all Christians that, be they Jews or Gentiles, bond or free, they are all incorporated into one company and they all make but one body. The unity of this visible body and Church of Christ consists in that uniformity which all the several persons belonging to it possess by reason of that one Lord whose servants they all profess to be, that one faith which they all acknowledge, that one Baptism by which they are all initiated. The visible Church of Jesus Christ is, therefore, one in outward profession of those things that supernaturally pertain to the very essence of Christianity and are required in every particular Christian person. (III,1)

As becomes those who follow with all humility the ways of peace, we honor, reverence, and obey--second only to God Himself--the voice of God's Church within which we live. (V,71)

We exhort everyone to worship God everywhere. But we hold that no place is so good for the performance of worship by God's assembled people as the Church. (V,16)

The great multitude of true believers, however dispersed they may be from one another, are all of one body of which Christ is the head, one building, of which He is the cornerstone. As members of this body, they are knit together. As stones of the building they are joined and used to build the Temple of the Lord. ... Those who are inwardly lively members of this body and polished stones of this building, coupled and joined to Christ as flesh of His flesh and bone of His bone, are linked and fastened to each other by the mutual bond of His unspeakable love towards them, their uncontrived faith in Him, and their sincere and hearty affection for one another. (First Sermon on Jude)

God put all things under Christ's feet and appointed Him to head His Church--Christ's very body--which is filled with Him and fills everyone with Him. Later Christ will yield up to the hands of his Father the scepter with which He presides over the world. His authority on earth will cease when there is no longer any Church to govern. He now exercises this governance both as God and as man--as God, by His essential presence with all things, as man by cooperation with that which is essentially present. (V,55)

We are actually in God only since the time of our adoption into the body of His true Church, into the fellowship of His children. He knows and loves His

Church and thus those who are in it. Our being in Christ by God's eternal foreknowledge does not save us unless we are adopted into the fellowship of His saints in this world. We are in Christ only by our incorporation into the society that has Him as their head and, together with Him, make a single body sharing a single name. (V,56)

Those who belong to the mystical body of our Savior Christ, the Church, are as numerous as the stars and are divided into many generations but nevertheless all joined to Christ as their head. Each particular person is joined to each other person because the same spirit that animated the blessed soul of our Savior Christ unites and creates His whole people, just as if He and they were so many limbs fashioned into one body and quickened by the same soul. (V,56)

Since the only subject which distinguishes ours from other religions is Jesus Christ, who none but the Church believes in and worships, we discover that the Apostles everywhere distinguish the Church from infidels and Jews by considering all who call upon the name of our Lord Jesus Christ to be in the Church. If we go deeper and try to define the Church more precisely, we will only add certain variable and incidental properties that are not of the essence of the Church but only make it a happier and more congenial society, either in fact or in the fanciful opinions of some people. (V,68)

The Church of God may contain both those who are not His, but must be taken by us as His because we do not know their inner thoughts, and those whose outward wickedness testifies to the whole world that God abhors them. (V,68)

Our critics do not define the Church in terms of what the Church essentially is but in terms of their own church, which they imagine to be more perfect than all the rest are. (V,68)

We must always remember that the Church has never fallen into tempestuous storms the clouds of which were not first seen to be rising from coldness of affection and neglect of the duty to worship God. If all the tears of the past that have been spilled over this matter could be seen, they would surely be sufficient to soften a heart of steel. (V,76)

The best things in the Church have been overthrown, not so much by the power and might of adversaries of the Church as through errors in judgment by those who should have upheld and defended the Church. (V,79)

That which each person should be inwardly, the Church should express outwardly. (V,6)

How can we come into the house of prayer and not be moved by the very glory of the place? (V,25)

Everything that is expedient and necessary for the ordering of spiritual matters cannot, of course, be of ancient provenance. The Church, as a body that never dies, always has as much power to ordain what never has been practiced in the past as it does to ratify what has gone before. (V,8)

The end that is aimed at in setting down the outward form of all religious actions is the edification of the Church. Now people are edified either when their understanding is improved somewhat about the acts that it behooves all persons to consider, or when their hearts are moved by any suitable emotion, or when their minds are in any way stirred up to that reverence, devotion, attention, and due regard which seems necessary at these times. Therefore, for this purpose not only speech but also other sensible means have always been thought necessary--especially those means which are an object to the eye, the liveliest and the most comprehending sense of all the others and therefore the fittest to make a deep and strong impression. From hence have risen not only a number of prayers, readings, questionings, exhortations, but also visible signs which, being used in the performance of holy actions, are undoubtedly most effectual to reveal such matters. (IV,1)

We would wish it understood that where neither the evidence of any divine law, nor the strength of any invincible contrary argument discovered by the light of reason, nor any notable public inconvenience is caused by our church laws--even when they have been only recently established--then the authority of the church alone is sufficient for ordering the services of worship and related practices. (V,8)

Churches: Dedication And Furnishings

There are those who maintain that the mere presence of a group of Christians gathered to worship makes their assembly a church, even as the presence of the king and his retinue will turn any house into a court. But I take this to be an error in judgment. The only thing that can make a place a church is the public and official designation of it as such. As for the mere presence of people gathered there in an assembly or the mere evidence of worship being performed, these do not, in themselves, infuse the place with any holiness. (V,12)

Has God anywhere said that it is His delight to dwell in a beggarly house or that He takes pleasure in being worshipped only in poor cottages? In the earliest days, the Lord was as acceptably honored by His people as He ever would be when the most stately places and worthy objects in the whole world were sought out as the locations and adornments of His temple. This great and beautiful building was only suitable, decent, and fitting for the greatness of Jesus Christ and solemnity of His Gospel--as would have been any estimable work of art. (V,15)

The solemn dedication of churches not only serves to make them authorized places of worship, but also transfers to God any right to them that their founders might otherwise claim, and makes God Himself the sole owner of the church. (V,12)

By offering such rich gifts to God we give testimony of our cheerful affection in thinking that nothing we possess is too valuable to be given for the furnishing and equipping of places of holy worship. In this way, we also give witness to the world of the might and power of Him whom we outwardly honor with our finest riches. Furthermore, wouldn't it be strange if God made such a store of glorious elements like gold, silver, and the like only to have them all consumed in secular vanity, allowing nothing but baser elements to be used in His own service? To display the majesty of kings, who are God's vice-regents in this world, we procure the rarest and most gorgeous treasures on earth. Do we think that God will accept only what the poorest of his kings would reject? (V,15)

When churches are denied their due pre-eminence and honor by not being properly sanctified, they seem to mourn as if injured and defrauded of their proper status. (V,16)

Of course, the true worship of God is in itself acceptable to Him because He cares not so much where it takes place as with what sincerity He is worshipped. Nevertheless, the majesty and holiness of the place of worship can have a good impact on **us** when it has the emotional effect of stirring up devotion and enhancing even our best and holiest acts of worship. (V,16)

—— Churches: Governance ——

Does it follow that everything we do in the Church, from the most to the least important, is unholy simply because the Lord Himself did not specifically institute it? By this reasoning, there is nothing holy that the Church, by her own authority, has prescribed and all ordinary laws that were ever made by ecclesiastical authority concerning spiritual matters are profane and unholy. (V,20)

Since the Church is a political society, it cannot possibly lack the power of providing for itself. And the major part of that power consists in the authority of making laws. Since corporations are perpetual, the laws of the ancient Church must necessarily bind the later Church so long as they are in force. But we must further note that because the Church remains the same, it still has the same authority and so may abrogate old laws or make new ones if the need arises. Therefore, appeal to ancient Canons and Constitutions as laws is in vain when they have either been secretly allowed to die by disuse or when they have been openly abrogated by contrary laws. (VII,14)

The spiritual power of the Church is such that it can neither be challenged by the right of nature nor be instituted by human authority, for the forces and effects of it are supernatural and divine.... I therefore conclude that spiritual authority is a power that Christ has given to be used over those who are subject to it for the good of their souls, according to Christ's own most sacred laws and the wholesome positive constitutions of His Church. (VI,2)

Just as it cannot be denied that the natural power to make laws resides in the commonwealth, we affirm that in a similar way the true original subject of power to make church laws is the whole entire body of that Church for which they are made. Equals cannot impose laws and statutes upon their equals. Therefore, no single person can impose ecclesiastical canon upon another; nor can a single Church impose such legislation upon another. If at any time they go about doing so, they must either show some kind of commission sufficient for their warrant or else be justly condemned for presumption in the sight both of God and humans. But nature itself abundantly authorizes the Church to make laws and orders for her children who are within her. For since every whole thing is naturally of greater power than any single part thereof, that which a whole Church ordains may with good reason be judged as having more weight than the will of any single individual or group of individuals within the compass of the same Church, and so may bind all to strict obedience. (VIII,6)

The Church as a supernatural society differs from natural societies in this: the persons with whom we associate ourselves in the latter are people simply considered as human, but those to whom we are joined in the other are God, angels, and holy people. Again, the Church is both a society and a supernatural society. Insofar as it is a society, it has the self same original grounds that other political societies have, namely, the natural inclination which all people have for social life and the consent they give to some certain bond of association that is the law that appoints the kind of order that they shall be associated in. Yet insofar as the Church is a supernatural society, this much is peculiar: that part of the bond of their association which belongs to the Church of God must be a supernatural law which God Himself has revealed concerning that kind of worship which His people shall offer Him. The substance of the worship of God, therefore, insofar as it has in it anything more than the law of reason teaches, may not be invented by men, as it is among the heathen, but must be received from God Himself, as it always has been in the Church, except when the Church has been forgetful of her duty. (I,15)

—— *Common (Corporate) Prayer* ——

If it is true that angels have their continual intercourse between the throne of God in Heaven and His Church here on earth, where could we find this more verified than in those two ghostly exercises: the one, *doctrine*, and the other, *prayer*? For what is the assembling of the Church to learn but the receiving of angels descending from above? And what is it to pray but to send angels upward? God's heavenly inspirations and our holy desires are like so many angels of intercourse and commerce between God and us. (V,23)

Our religious life begins and ends with prayer. We on earth have little knowledge about things done in heaven but we know that the saints in heaven pray. Because prayer is something common to the Church triumphant and is a work that we share with the angels, we think that much of our lives can be celestial and divine to the extent that we spend them in the exercise of prayer. (V,23)

Public common prayer is not like private prayer. In private prayer secrecy is commended rather than outward expression. Common prayer is a public act of a whole community and thus pays more attention to the external appearance of the service. (V,25)

Our service of prayer as a public body is common prayer. Because it is corporate and public, it must be considered much worthier than private prayer even as public society is more important than any one person within it. (V,24)

When we make our prayers in common it must be that we do so with more assurance than when we pray in private. The things we ask for publicly have been approved as necessary and good by the judgment of everyone and we hear them sought after and desired with common consent. If our own zeal and devotion toward God is slack, we are supported, enhanced, and spurred on by the alertness and fervor of others. (V,24)

The good we do by common prayer is greater than can be accomplished in private prayer, not only because we receive more benefit from it ourselves, but also because the whole Church is strengthened by our good example. (V,24)

God may add other uses to His sanctuary, either by His ordinance or by His special allowance and goodness, but the principal reason for its existence must be common prayer. (V,25)

A great part of the reason why religious minds are so inflamed with the love of public corporate worship is the force and efficacy that they discover through experience with the very form and reverend solemnity of properly ordered common prayer. (V,25)

Common prayer helps us to overcome the weakness and ignorance that makes us less able to perform the heavenly worship of God with the affection of heart and disposition of soul that is necessary. (V,25)

Of all the aids for the proper performance of common prayer the greatest is the very regularity and prescription of both form and content in the service. (V,25)

No doubt our worship service came from God. We must acknowledge it to be the result of His special care and generosity that the Church would forever have a prescribed form of common prayer which, though not the same in all respects everywhere, nevertheless, for the most part has the same general form. (V,25)

If prayers were in no other way acceptable to God except when they are newly conceived according to the needs of the present moment...if prayers are actions that are to dissipate as soon as they are said, if prayers that are once made and then used over again are seen as only instruments of superstition, then surely we cannot excuse Moses who gave scandal to the world by not being content to praise Almighty God with typical simplicity of spirit for the admirable victory that God gave the Jews over Pharaoh. Moses cast his prayers in a poetical fashion that could be repeated often in the future even though there would never again be exactly the same event that had called them forth in the first place. (V,26)

The time we spend in our service on praying and reading enables the person who prays to be more attentive in listening and the person who listens more earnest in praying. (V,34)

How could the Church ever have devised something more proper and convenient than that, when all of us together have received these heavenly mysteries wherein Christ gave Himself to us, and when we have given visible testimony of our blessed communion with Him, we should, out of hatred of all heresies, factions, and schism--with the pastor as our leader and we as willing followers--openly declare ourselves united as brethren in one body? We do this in such a way that every petition, even if it does not require it, is always conveyed by a multitude of persons speaking simultaneously. (V,36)

—— *The Commonwealth (Christian)* ——

True religion is the root of all true virtue and the foundation off all well-ordered commonwealths. (V,1)

If the course of public affairs cannot in any good manner proceed without effective human participation, and if that which enables people are their virtues, then let government acknowledge its debt to religion. (V,1)

Religion, when truly embraced, directs people's behavior toward all sorts of virtuous service to the commonwealth. (V,1)

He who goes about to persuade a multitude that they are not so well governed as they ought to be will never lack attentive and favorable listeners (I,1).

Pure and unstained religion ought to be the highest goal of public governance. This is because of the force that religion has to instruct all sorts of people to make them serviceable in public affairs: governors, to make them more likely to rule with conscience; ordinary people, to make them more willing, in good conscience, to obey the laws. (V,1)

Students of public policy have taught consistently that commonwealths are founded upon laws and that only by a general acceptance of these laws, which keep them in order, can a people be formed into a single body politic. (Discourse on Justification)

If all who believe are contained by the name "Church," how should the Church be differentiated from the commonwealth when the whole commonwealth believes? The Church and the commonwealth therefore are in this case one society. This society is called a commonwealth insofar as it lives under whatever its particular form of secular law and rule may be, and the Church insofar as it follows the spiritual law of Jesus Christ. For, since these two laws contain so many and such different offices, there must of necessity be appointed some in it who have one charge and some the other, yet without dividing the whole and making it into two different and separated societies. (VIII,1)

The ground of all civil law is this: *No one ought to be hurt or injured by another.* Take away this agreement and you take away all laws. Take away all laws and what becomes of commonwealths? (Discourse on Justification)

Things of general benefit may always be incommodious, by some accident or other, to a few people. For what in this world is so perfect that no inconvenience ever results from it? In these cases there are private remedies for private problems but this must not disrupt the general welfare. (V,6)

We hold that there is not any person who is a member of the Church of England who is not also a member of the English Commonwealth nor any member of the commonwealth who is not also a member of the Church of England. Therefore, just as a triangle has a base…and yet one and the self same line is both a base and a side-- simply a side but also a base if it happens to be the bottom and underlie the others--just so, properties and actions of one kind can cause the name of commonwealth while properties and functions of the other cause the name Church to be given to a multitude of people. Yet one and the self same multitude exist in such a way, as it is with us, that no person may be a member of the one without also being a member of the other. (VIII,1)

We must note that members of a Christian commonwealth have a triple status: <u>natural</u>, <u>civil</u>, and <u>spiritual</u>. (VIII,1)

We grant that a Church and a commonwealth are things distinguished in nature from one another; commonwealth is defined in one way, Church in another.…Every political body has some religion, but the Church has that religion which is true. Truth in religion is what properly distinguishes the Church from other political societies of human beings.… And the Church of Jesus Christ is every political society of humans that holds that religious truth that is proper to Christianity. It maintains religion as a political society; as a Church, it maintains that religion which God has revealed in Jesus Christ. Therefore, with us the name "church" means only a society of human beings united into some public form of regiment that is distinguished from other societies by the exercise of Christian religion. (VIII,1)

Therefore, the Church and the commonwealth are in our case only one society. This society is called a commonwealth insofar as it lives under some form of secular law and regiment; it is called a church insofar as it follows the spiritual law of Jesus Christ. For both of these laws contain so many and different kinds of offices that there must of necessity be appointed in it some to one charge and some to another, yet without dividing the whole and making it two different and impaled societies. (VIII,1)

The gross and stupid idea of those who lack understanding is that those with the fullest bellies are the happiest. The greatest felicity such people wish for the commonwealth in which they live is that it will flourish and endure, that those who are riotous may have power without limit, that the poor may sleep and the rich feed them, that nothing unpleasant will be commanded and nothing forbidden those who pursue their own lusts, that kings may provide for the ease of their subject and not be too curious about their behavior, that wanton excess and lewd living will be allowed, and that no fault will be regarded as important except disapproval of all of the above. Far be it that the just should dwell near the tents of these miserable felicities! (V,76)

Everyone agrees that the natural subject of civil power is the body of the commonwealth. The good or evil estate of the commonwealth depends so much upon the power of making laws that in all well settled states, even if they are monarchies, there must be perpetual diligence to guarantee that the commonwealth does not completely resign herself and turn this power over into the hands of any single person. This is why William, whom we call the Conqueror, having made war against England in the name of his title to the crown, knew that as the inheritor thereof he could not lawfully change the laws of the land by himself. For the English commonwealth had not invested her previous kings with the fullness of so great a power. Therefore, William took the style and title of a conqueror. (VIII,6)

The Parliament of England, along with the Convocation of the Church that is joined to it, is that body upon which the very essence of all government within this kingdom depends. It is the body of the whole realm; it consists of the king and of all in the land who are subject to him; for they were all present there either in person, or represented by those persons to whom they voluntarily assigned their very personal rights. (VIII,6)

In a church that is well ordered, the king, as supreme magistrate, is responsible for seeing that the laws of God concerning His worship and all other affairs and orders of the Church are executed and duly observed. The chief magistrate is also responsible for seeing that ecclesiastical persons perform the duty of their appointed offices, and for punishing those who fail in those offices. In a word, it belongs to the earthly power that God has given the chief magistrate to defend the laws of the Church, to cause them to be executed, and to punish their transgressors. On all sides, therefore, it is confessed that to the king belongs the power of enforcing laws made for the Church's governance and of causing them to be obeyed. (VIII,6)

Confession (See Also Absolution)

Could there be anything better devised than that all of us, at our first access to God in prayer, should acknowledge meekly our sins and do so not only in our hearts but with our voices so that all present are ear-witnesses to one another's distinct and deliberate assent to each part of the common indictment drawn up against us? (V,36)

As for private confession and absolution, it stands as follows with us: we teach and profess that the minister has the power of absolution. The Church is not denied the authority either of abridging or enlarging the use and exercise of that power. No obligation is imposed upon the people to confess their transgressions to other persons, as though the remission of sins were otherwise impossible. ... In this regard, the Church of England has always thought it the safer way to refer peoples' secret crimes only to God and themselves. A word of special caution, however, should be extended to those who come to the Holy Sacrament, and to those who are ready to depart from the world. (VI,4)

Confirmation

The Fathers of the Church have always imputed to Confirmation the gift or grace of the Holy Spirit not to make us Christians in the first instance, but to assist us with all goodness and arm us against temptation and sin after we have been made Christians in Baptism. (V,66)

In expectation of Confirmation, baptized children were seasoned with the principles of true religion before malice and corrupt examples depraved their minds. A good foundation was laid for the direction of their entire lives, the seed of the Church of God was preserved in a sincere and reliable way, and bishops and godfathers, to whom the care of their souls belonged, saw to it that, by testing and examining them, some of their own heavy burden was discharged. (V,66)

Only bishops, as successors to the Apostles, have had this power of laying-on-of-hands. Nowhere has it appeared that anyone else has had these miraculous gifts and graces that God was pleased to offer His Church. (V,66)

It was never the intention of the Church to say that it was absolutely impossible to receive the Holy Ghost in the sacrament of Baptism without the later addition of the laying on of hands in Confirmation by a bishop. Rather, because the integrity of the Church depended on the dignity of her superiors, it seemed reasonable and fit to honor bishops by giving them certain powers not given to others. Without such pre-eminence in bishops, there would be as many schisms as there were priests. (V,66)

— *Conquest* —

Some peoples are brought into subjection by force.… It pleases their conquerors to lay upon them that yoke of subjection which they are entitled to impose by just and lawful wars. Conquerors hold their power over such multitudes as a thing descending to them from divine providence itself. For it is God who gives victory in the day of war and dominion of this kind is derived from Him. Conquerors enjoy the same right by the law of nations, which authorizes them to reign as absolute lords over those whom they vanquish. Sometimes it pleases God by special appointment to select and nominate those to whom dominion shall be given. He often did this in the Commonwealth of Israel. Those who receive power in this way have it immediately from God by simple divine right. Others have this dominion by human right determined by human discretion when people are left free by God to make a choice of their own governor. (VIII,2)

—— *Consent* ——

The general and perpetual voice of people is as the sentence of God himself. For that which all people have at all times learned, nature herself must necessarily have taught. And God, being the author of nature, her voice is but His instrument. (I,8)

—— *Constitutional Monarchy* ——

I am not of the opinion that to place the greatest possible limitations on the power of kings is the best idea, either for them or for the people; there should, rather, be only the best sort of limitation of the king's power. The most fully limited power is that which permits kings to have authority over the fewest things, while the best sort of limitation is that which limits their acts to the most sound, perfect, and impartial rule, which is the rule of law. I refer here not only to the law of nature and of God but to every national or municipal law which is consonant with those two. (VIII,3)

Happier that people whose law is the king…Where the king guides the state and the law guides the king, that commonwealth is like a harp or melodious instrument, the strings of which are tuned and handled by a single hand which follows as laws the rules and canons of musical science…. In this respect, I cannot but choose to commend highly the wisdom of those who laid the foundations of this English Commonwealth where, even though no person or cause is excused from subjection to the king's power, the power of the king over all and in all is limited, since the law itself is a rule that limits all of his proceedings. (VIII,3)

The axioms of our royal government are: *lex facit regem* ("The law makes the king"). The king's grant of any favor made contrary to law is void; *rex nihil potest, nisi quod jure potest* ("The king is not empowered to do anything, unless he is empowered by the law"). Therefore, when our kings take possession of the office to which they are called, they are shown by the very solemnities and rites of their inauguration what affairs the law gives them authority over and the limits of their power. They are crowned, enthroned, and anointed. The crown they wear is a sign of leadership over the military; the throne they sit upon is a sign of sitting in judgment; the oil that anoints them is a symbol of religious or sacred power. (VIII,3)

The internal well being of a commonwealth is thought to depend upon nothing more than upon these two special affections: fear and love--fear of the king by the subjects and love by the king for the subjects who live under him. The love of subjects continues, for the most part, to last as long as the righteousness of the king lasts and as long as their virtue does not decay. Such righteousness and virtue endure as long as kings fear to do that which might alienate the loving hearts of their subjects from them. Fear to do evil grows from the harm that evildoers will suffer. (VIII,9)

Kings do not all have equal latitude in their power of dominion. Kings by conquest make their own charter so that we cannot with any certainty define further how great is their power, either civil or spiritual. We can only set them within the bounds of the general laws of God and nature. Those who are kings by God's own special appointment also have all the power that God has assigned or permitted with His approval. With regard to kings who were first instituted by agreement made with those over whom they reign concerning how far their power may lawfully extend, the article of agreement between them must show not only the original articles of their compact (which for the most part are either completely forgotten or else known to very few) but also whatever has been freely and voluntarily accepted either by express consent, as evidenced in written laws or else, by silent acceptance--as famously notified through custom reaching back beyond the memory of men and women. (VIII,3)

— *Contrition* —

Belief in the world to come and in the judgment to come, faith in the promises and sufferings of Christ for humankind, fear of His majesty, love of His mercy, grief for sin, hope of pardon, seeking grace--all these we know to be the elements of true contrition. (VI,6)

Contrition is not a natural passion or anguish which arises to thwart our wills. It is rather a deliberate aversion of the human will from sin, an aversion always accompanied by grief. This grief is sometimes accompanied with tears and often with other external signs. For this reason it has sometimes been thought that contrition consists mostly of these things. But the principal element in contrition is that alteration whereby the will, which was before delighted with sin, now abhors and shuns nothing more. But since we cannot hate sin in ourselves without the depression and grief that is caused by the hatefulness of the thing within us, the will averted from sin must necessarily make the acceptable motion suitable.… So repentance must begin with a truly sorrowful heart, a sorrow that rends the heart--neither feigned nor slight. Such sorrow is not feigned lest it increase sin nor slight, lest the pleasures of sin overpower it. (VI,3)

— *Cosmopolitanism* —

Human nature is more content living within civil society than in any kind of private solitary living because the benefits of mutual participation are so much greater in society. Even here we are not satisfied because we covet a kind of society and fellowship with all of humankind. Socrates intended to signify this when he professed himself a citizen, not of this or that commonwealth, but of the world. The effect of that very natural desire in us (a manifest token that we wish for a sort of universal fellowship with all humans) appears by the wonderful delight some people have in visiting foreign countries, and others in discovering nations not heard of in former ages. We all like to know the affairs and dealings of other people, yea to be in a bond of friendship with them. And we desire this not only the sake of traveling, or so that confederation with others might make each stronger, but for the same urge that moved the Queen of Sheba to visit Solomon (1 Kings 10:1). (I,10)

—— *Creed (Apostle's)* ——

From the Apostles and our Lord Jesus Christ we have received that short confession of faith that has always been a badge for the Church, a mark by which to distinguish Christians from infidels and Jews. (V,42)

The Creed is a most divine explication of the major parts of our Christian faith. (V,42)

—— *Cross (Sign Of)* ——

The cross is an admonition, no less necessary today than in the past, that we are to glory in the service of Jesus Christ and not hang our heads in shame, even if we are reproached and disgraced for doing so at the hands of this wretched world. (V,65)

There is a clear and important difference between honoring the cross superstitiously, as if it were Christ

Himself, and the ceremony of the cross, which serves only as a symbol of remembrance. (V,65)

Shall I say that making the sign of the cross, as we do, is in some way a means to assure our preservation from God's reproach? Once this idea enters the palace of our imagination, none of us Christians could ever desire a more effective, though silent, teacher to help us avoid whatever may deservedly lead to our fall from grace. (V,65)

In those things of which we should be ashamed, we are admonished by the sign of the cross at the very moment when admonishment is most needed. (V,65)

The surest bond that ties us in obedience to Christ, the most solemn vow that we ever made to obey him, was a promise made in Baptism. Among other reminders of that vow we cannot think that the sign of the cross, made on our newly baptized foreheads, is either unsuitable or ineffective. (V,65)

It is not, you may say, the cross we make on our foreheads but the faith in Christ that is in our hearts that arms us with patience, constancy and courage. Even though we grant that this is very true, we dare not discard even the smallest help that furthers, even in the slightest way, the high services that God requires at our hands. If anyone denies that such ceremonies are useful at least as reminders of his duty, or thinks that he, personally, has no need to be reminded, it is still reasonable for us to think that the general experience of the whole world outweighs such an opinion when it is held by only a few people. In any event, the rare perfection of a few should bow to the common need. (V,65)

— *Crucifixion (Passion)* —

I foolishly labor here to explain what cannot really be explained. Our best response to this awful mystery is an amazed silence. (Sermon on Proverbs/Matthew/Hebrews)

In our Savior's death is combined the highest degree of honor and the lowest degree of humiliation. (Sermon on Proverbs/Matthew/Hebrews)

God's rejection of Christ [on the cross] was only of His human nature. It affected only his body and the part of His soul wherein His passions and emotions resided. The intellectual part of Jesus' soul, the part where reason, judgment, wisdom, the comprehension of truth, the light of God shone, could not possibly be extinguished. (Sermon on Proverbs/Matthew/Hebrews)

When Christ cries out, "My God, my God," the strong sinews of His words and the force and vigor of His speech show us that He has clasped God with a fast embrace, and that God already abides in His fortress-- the very pinnacle and turret of Christ's soul. (Sermon on Proverbs/Matthew/Hebrews)

At this hour, neither God, nor angels, nor man came to ease His heavy heart with the comfort of their presence. Instead, a curtain was drawn between the passionate powers of His soul and whatever might bring Him relief and refreshment. ... Who can hear the mournful cry of Christ and not feel that his own soul has been scorched without leaving a single drop of the moisture of joyful feeling? (Sermon on Proverbs/Matthew/Hebrews)

Let us weigh Christ's words when He said, "My soul is now troubled and what should I say: Father save me from this hour? But for this cause I came to this hour." His purpose here was effectively to propose to the world two contrary goals the like of which--in power and efficacy--had never before been presented in that way to anyone except Christ Himself. Presented before His eyes in that fearful hour was, on the one hand, God's terrible indignation and wrath toward mankind--a wrath as yet unappeased--death still in full strength, hell not yet mastered by anyone who had heretofore come within its borders and confines, and yet more horrors than it is probably either possible or necessary for the mind of man to uncover. All of this He was left alone to engage and battle in His flesh-and-blood nature. (V,48)

On the other side was a world waiting to be saved, a pacification of God's wrath awaiting the dignity of that sacrifice that would not allow His tabernacle to be corrupted, and the utter disappointment of all the infernal powers of hell that had Him in their hands but could not touch Him because of the purity of His soul. No one should marvel that in such a circumstance the soul of Christ was much troubled. What would such apprehension breed but inexplicable passions--desires that abhorred what they embraced and embraced what they abhorred? In this agony how would the tongue go about expressing what the soul was enduring? (V,48)

Concerning death in itself, surely nature taught Christ to avoid it. Concerning death as a means to procure the salvation of the world, His mercy worked within Him a complete willingness of mind to accept death. In these two desires--these two prayers--there is not repugnant contradiction. The death of Christ, in itself, was not God's purpose. He willed and allowed it to happen so that we might thereby obtain life. (V,48)

— *Death* —

Death is something that everyone suffers, but not everyone approaches it with the same attitude or in the same way. Being necessarily something common, death is, through the manifold persuasions, dispositions, and occasions of persons equally deserving of praise or condemnation, shunned by some and desired by others. We cannot absolutely disparage or approve either the willingness to live or the inclination to die. (V,46)

There is some good reason why a virtuous mind might wish to depart this world with a kind of gradual dissolution rather than to be cut off suddenly in an instant. (V,46)

Let us beg God that when the hour of our rest has come the patterns of our dissolution will be like Jacob, Moses, Joshua, or David, who peacefully and at some leisure ended their lives while praying for the mercies of God to come upon their posterity. They were able to replenish the hearts of those closest to them with words of immeasurable consolation and to strengthen others in fear of God, while giving them wholesome instruction about life, confirming them in true religion, and, in sum, teaching the world how to die virtuously, even as they had taught them earlier how to live. (V,46)

Whether we consider evil people or good people, whether we think of ourselves or of others, to be preserved from sudden death is a blessing from God. Our prayer against sudden death carries with it a twofold desire: first, that when death comes it gives us some time to get ready; secondly, that if God denies us that wish, we may still have the wisdom to have provided for all necessary things ahead of time so that those misfortunes that careless people suffer because of unexpected death will not affect us and, in this sense, though death may be sudden in itself, it will not really be sudden because we have prepared for it. (V,46)

Usually it is for virtuous considerations that wisdom may prevail and make us desire a slow and deliberate death, contrary to our natural inclinations. In such cases we are content to endure the longer period of grief and bodily pain so that the soul may have time to call itself to account for past deeds and for full repentance. This is a time in which to exercise patience so that the joys of the kingdom have time to present themselves and there is time for the pleasures of sin and the vanities of this world to be censured with an uncorrupted judgment, time to decide where the last seeds of charity may most faithfully be bestowed, time for the mind to weigh carefully how best to dispose of worldly things that it can never change afterwards. (V,46)

There is nothing that the soul desires so much in the final hour as comfort against the natural terrors of death and other scruples of conscience that commonly trouble and perplex the weak at this time. The law of God exacts from our hands all the help that Christian forgiveness and indulgence can offer such people. Our major consolation, as we depart this life, is the hope of that glorious and blessed resurrection to which the Apostle Paul referred when he said that, just as all will be raised again from the dead, the just shall be taken up and exalted above the rest. (V,68)

The Lord Himself was not reluctant to register in the Book of Life how His servants ended their days on earth. He condescended to their smallest actions such as what food they wanted during their final illness, what they said to their children, family and friends, where they willed their dead bodies to be laid, how they framed their last wills and testaments, even to the turning of their dead faces to this side or that, the degrees by which their natural heat had departed them, their cries, their groans, their pantings, breathings and last gaspings. He has most solemnly commended all of these details to the memory of all generations. (Sermon on Remedy Against Fear and Sorrow)

Because death still has the upper hand against all of us, it is natural to fear it. (Sermon on Proverbs/Matthew/Hebrews)

The best weapon we have to strike back against the natural terrors of death is the submission we owe to God's will, at Whose commandment our readiness to die shows that we are called from this stage of life as His sons and daughters, not as servants. Those who lived as His children, being dead, are blessed. The pains that they suffered here are now ended; the evil that they did is buried with them; their good works follow them. Not even their bodies are lost but are laid up for them. (Sermon on Proverbs/Matthew/Hebrews)

We see by daily experience that some people, as the hour of death approaches, as they hear themselves summoned to appear and stand at the bar of the Judge whose brightness causes the eyes of the angels themselves to be dazzled, begin to hide the faces of their idle imaginations. To name their merits at such a time is to lay their souls upon the rack. The memory of their deeds is then loathsome to them. They forsake everything in which they had previously put their trust and confidence.

There is no staff to lean upon, no ease, no rest, no comfort then, except Christ Jesus. (Discourse on Justification)

— *Demons* —

We know that some of the angels of God have fallen.… It seems that there was no other way for angels to sin except by self-awareness of their goodness. When they began to admire themselves for their sublimity and honor, the memory of their subordination and dependence on God was drowned. When this happened their adoration, love and imitation of God could not help but be interrupted. The fall of the angels was pride. (I,4)

Since their fall, the practices of the angels have been completely contrary of those mentioned before. For, some being dispersed in the air, some on the earth, some in the water, some among the minerals, dens and caves that are under the earth, they have by all means possible labored to effect a universal rebellion against the laws and, as far as in them lies, the utter destruction of the works of God. These wicked spirits the heathen honored as gods, both generally under the name of *Dii inferi*, infernal gods, and more particularly, some in oracles, some in idols, some as household gods, some as nymphs. In a word, there was no foul and wicked spirit that was not in one way or another honored by humans as God, until such time as light appeared in the world and dissolved the works of the Devil. (I,4)

— *Depression (Despair And Grief)* —

We would not know delight and joy if we did not also have a healthy intercourse with the darkness of despair. Too much honey turns to gall and too much joy, even spiritual joy, will make us immoral, malicious and willful. Happier by far is that person whose soul is humbled with inner desolation than he whose heart is puffed up and exalted beyond all reason by an abundance of spiritual delights. (Sermon on Certainty of Faith)

Better sometimes to go down into the pit with one, who beholding the darkness and bewailing the loss of inner joy and consolation, says from the bottom of lowest hell, "My God, my God, why have You forsaken me?" rather than continually to walk arm and arm with angels and to sit, as it were, in the bosom of Abraham and have no doubt and no thought except, "I thank God it is not with me as it is with other men," (Sermon on Certainty of Faith).

Our God will have those who are to walk in light feel from time to time what it is to sit in the shadow of death. A grieving spirit is, therefore, no excuse for a faithless mind. (Sermon on Certainty of Faith)

By nature, we seek safety from harm. Things that are harmful in the present moment breed depression in us; if anticipated as future events, they cause fear. To abate the one, our Savior said to His disciples, "Let not your hearts be troubled." To moderate the other, He added, "Fear not." (Sermon on Remedy Against Sorrow and Fear)

It is not true, as the Stoics claim, that it is unseemly for a wise man to be affected with grief of mind; but it is unwise to be sorrowful and depressed without cause--to lament when we should rejoice. ... [For example] we err when we grieve at a wicked person's pride and prosperity because, rightly understood, they neither prosper nor go unpunished. (Sermon on Remedy Against Sorrow and Fear)

Even though the cause of our depression is reasonable, we should not yield to it with too much self-indulgence. … Whenever depression occurs it troubles and unsettles the mind. Therefore, whether we are moved vainly by that which seems harmful but is not or have just cause for grief because we are confronted by harmful events, our Savior's teaching is to "be not troubled" in the first case and to be not overly troubled in the second. For, although to have no feelings about what oppresses us is stupid, nevertheless, since the Author of our Salvation was Himself consecrated by affliction, the path by which we are to follow Him is not strewn with rushes but paved with thorns. (Sermon on Remedy Against Sorrow and Fear)

⸻ *Devil (Satan)* ⸻

The sin of the Devil comes originally from himself, the sin of people from the Devil's instigation.…The sin of the Devil is pride, and, arising from pride, unbelief.…The Devil is the father of lying, that is, of infidelity and sin in others.… Is man then to be excused? By no means, for the Devil sows the seed of sin but each person's concupiscence receives it, foments it, brings it forth. Each person's will is the true cause of sin; the Devil merely sets it in motion and urges it. (Notes Toward a Fragment on Predestination)

Satan and his imps were permitted [by God] to beat upon Christ's body like an anvil and to assault His senses with whatever wit and malice they could invent. His eyes they wounded with the spectacle of scornful looks, His ears with the sound of heinous blasphemies, His taste with gall, the feeling throughout His body with such tortures as blows, thorns, whit, nails and spear could breed, until His soul was finally chased out of Him like a bird. (Sermon on Proverbs/Matthew/Hebrews)

From Satan's forge and nowhere else has come the strange notion that to worship God with a set form of common prayer is superstitious, as if God Himself had not framed for his priests the exact words with which He charged them to bless the people. Did not our Lord, in order to prevent this practice of extemporaneous and voluntary prayer, leave us His own set prayer to remain as a part of the liturgy and serve a pattern by which to frame other prayers? (V,26)

— *Doubt* —

Although God's goodness to us in His reconciling love is so great that we cannot measure it by the number of hours, days, and years of our lives, if we put all His acts together they lack the force to overcome the doubt that comes from the fear of losing a tiny transitory favor from our fellows, or some other small calamity. We immediately imagine that we are crossed clean out of God's book, that He favors others and does not love us, and that He has passed us by like a stranger who no longer knows us. (Sermon on Certainty of Faith).

— *Equity* —

Equity is not contrary to law; it is above it, binding our consciences in ways to which law can never aspire. (V,9)

The voice of equity and justice proclaims that a general law never undermines a special privilege unless that privilege limits the force of the law, in which case the general law overturns the privilege. (V,81)

General laws in religion and politics are like general laws in medicine. No one wants to be treated for a disease by a remedy that may work well in others who have his illness if he has some other condition attached to his disease that will react badly to that remedy. Such a treatment will be harmful for him, or at least useless. So, we must not, because of the lustrous authority of the holy laws of the Church, or because of all the good reasons why such laws will serve the common good, imagine that there is only one standard to fit every situation. (V,9)

Even though the general course of common affairs should be governed by general rules, it is fair to consider particular exigencies and practical circumstances as allowable exceptions to such general rules. (V,9)

Since all good laws are the voices of right reason, which is God's instrument for guiding the world, and since it is impossible that right can stand against right, it must follow that principles and rules of justice intend--whether or not they expressly declare it--to allow exceptions to their application in those particular situations where a literal imposition of their force would be inequitable. (V,9)

The hand of justice must distribute what is due in each particular case and make this judgment with no less regard for the particular circumstances than for general

rules or axioms. This must be so because the v
qualities, and conditions of all sorts of people cannot be
fit under one standard. For example, common law binds
everyone to keep his promises, perform his agreements,
and keep the word given on his own behalf or that of
others. Nevertheless, he who bargains with someone who
is under-age can gain no benefit from a charge of breach
of contract because he brings the allegation against a
person who is exempt from the law. Special cases are
governed by special rules. (V,81)

Interpreted as a broad generality, a law would seem to
apply in the same way to all cases. But once we descend
to have a closer look, we see that each particular case
is not the same as each other case. General precepts
always presuppose perfect equality in all cases to which
they apply, but not such perfection that is unattainable,
for then we would be asking, in vain, that which people
cannot do. General precepts only imply that degree
of perfection that humans, with all possible help and
support, should try to achieve. (V,81)

—— *Eucharist (Holy Comunion)* ——

Those of us who would live the life of God must eat the
flesh and drink the blood of the Son of man because this
is that part of our diet without which we cannot live.
(V,67)

We know that His flesh is meat and His blood drink,
not by presumed imagination, but truly, so truly that
through faith we perceive in the body and blood of the
sacrament the very taste of eternal life. The grace of

the sacrament is present as the food we eat and drink. (V,67)

The real presence of Christ's most blessed body and blood is not, therefore, to be sought in the sacrament but in the worthy receiver of the sacrament. (V,67)

I do not see any conclusion we can draw from Christ's words about when and where the bread is his body or the cup His blood except that they are to be found in the heart and soul of the person who receives them. (V,67)

The fruit of the Eucharist is the *participation* of the body and blood of Christ in our hearts and lives. (V,67)

Nowhere in Scripture is there support for the idea, embraced strongly by some, that in the sacrament there is a literal, corporal, and oral transmission of the very substance of Christ's body and blood. (V,67)

Our duty is to take what is offered and rest in the assurance that if we eat the bread we are saved. (V,67)

often

Blessed and praised forever be God's name, who, knowing of what senseless and heavy metal we are made, has instituted in His Church a spiritual supper, a Holy Communion, to be celebrated often so that we might by that celebration have the frequent occasion to examine these spiritual buildings that we are to see what condition they are in. Since God does not dwell in temples that are unclean, we receive this Holy Supper as a seal, a promise, that we are His house, His sanctuary, that His Christ is as truly united to me as I am to Him--as surely as my arm is joined to my shoulder, that He dwells in me as surely as the elements of bread and wind abide within me; that by receiving these holy mysteries, I profess my faith. (Second Sermon on Jude)

Life ot World-Unity w/ Christ

Before we put forth our hands to take this blessed sacrament, we are charged to examine and test our hearts to see whether God is truly in us or not. (Second Sermon on Jude)

When we receive the sacrament of the Supper of the Lord in a spiritual way, is not all other wine like the water of Marah compared to this blessed cup? Is not manna like gall and our holy bread like manna? Is there not a taste of Christ Jesus in the heart of him who eats this Supper? Does not he who drinks behold plainly in this cup that his soul is bathed in the blood of the Lamb? Oh, beloved in our Lord and Savior Jesus Christ, if you would taste how sweet the Lord is, if you would receive the King of glory, then first build up yourselves in faith. (Second Sermon on Jude)

The principal thing that our Grand Deliverer would have us forever remember is that by death He wrought our deliverance. For this reason the sacrament of the Holy Eucharist was instituted so that the breaking of flesh and shedding of blood, that is to say, the very face of death, would appear within it. (Sermon on Proverbs/ Matthew/ Hebrews)

Seeing that Christ is in us as a quickening spirit, the first part of our communion with Him necessarily consists in the participation of His spirit with us. (V,56)

The bread and the wine are his body and blood because once we receive them they become the causes of the *participation* of His body and blood in them. Anything that produces a certain effect is not vainly or improperly said to be the effect that the thing intended to produce. Every cause is in the effect that grows from it. Our souls and bodies, when quickened to eternal life, are effects the cause of which is the very Person of Christ. His body and blood are the true wellspring out of which salvation flows. They are in the elements through which they give new life not only because of their result, in the way the influences of the heavens are in plants, animals, and humans, but also, by a far more divine and mystical kind of union that makes us one with Him even as He and the Father are one. (V,67)

Because the work of Christ's spirit within us is hindered by sin and death, which already possesses us, it was necessary, both for the sake of our present sanctification to new life and for the future resurrection of our bodies, that there be participation on our parts in Christ's grace, power, merit, and virtue as contained in his body and blood. (V,56)

As for any mixture of the substance of Christ's flesh with ours, the participation that we have of Christ allows no such gross surmise. (V,56)

This heavenly food is given to us for the filling of our empty souls and not for exercising our curiosity and our subtle minds. (V,67)

Whatever benefit the vital body and blood of Christ may yield, is received by steps and degrees until we have the full measure of divine grace and are sanctified and saved in the day of our final exaltation in a state of fellowship in heaven with Him whose partakers we now are. (V,56)

We receive Christ Jesus only once in Baptism as the origin of grace. In the Eucharist we receive Christ often as the ongoing completion of our lives. (V,57)

The grace that we receive from the Holy Eucharist does not begin life but continues it. No one may receive *or part of holy?*

this sacrament before he is baptized because no dead
thing is capable of nourishment. (V,67)

Considering the limited success that truth has
had in bitter conflicts with error on this question
[transubstantiation *versus* consubstantiation] should I
not wish that we would give ourselves more to meditate
in silence about what we are given in the sacrament and
to dispute less about how it is done? (V,67)

The person whose soul is possessed by this Pascal
Lamb and made joyful in the strength of this new wine
feels wonderful things, sees great sights, and utters
unheard sounds. This holy bread has in it more than
the substance that our eyes behold. This cup, hallowed
with solemn benediction, gives endless life and welfare
to both soul and body because it serves as both medicine
to heal our infirmities and purge our sins and a sacrifice
of thanksgiving, while at the same time it sanctifies and
enlightens us with faith and truly conforms us to the
image of Christ. (V,67)

—— *Excommunication (Censures)* ——

Excommunication indeed cuts a person off from the
Church, but not from the commonwealth. … The person
who before had fellowship with that society of which she
or he was a member with regard to things spiritual as well
as civil is by force of excommunication cut off for a time
from communion with those things that belong to the
body insofar as it is the Church but is not severed from
the same body insofar as it is concerned with civil affairs.
A person who has been both excommunicated by the
Church and deprived of dignity in the commonwealth

is, upon repentance, readmitted into the Church but not necessarily into the commonwealth. (VIII,1)

The power which our Savior gave to his Church is of two kinds: the one to be exercised only over voluntary penitents, the other over such as are to be brought to amendment by ecclesiastical censure.... In this latter kind of spiritual jurisdiction, where censures constrain people to amend their lives, the minister of God does no more than declare and signify what God has wrought. And it is true that the Church of God has this power invested in it. (VI,6)

Excommunications do not have either the nature of judicial punishments or the force of sufficient argument to prove that ecclesiastical judges should have authority to call their own Sovereign to appear before them in their consistories to be examined, judged, and excommunicated if found culpable. Excommunications are only dutiful, religious, and holy refusals to admit notorious transgressors to share in the communion of saints, and especially in the mysteries of the body and blood of Christ. We grant that every king is bound to accept that, until the minds of such transgressors become manifestly humbled and penitent, any minister of God has the right and duty of imposing such restrictions anywhere throughout the world. (VIII,9)

Since the kings of England are, within their own dominions, the highest authority and without peer, how is it possible that any civil or ecclesiastical court person under them should have coercive power over them, when such power would make that person his superior's ruler and judge? It cannot therefore stand with the nature of such sovereign rule that any subject should have power to exercise on kings the greatest censure of excommunication as this is allowed in the platform of the discipline of the Reformed Churches. For this reason, until better reason be offered to prove that kings cannot lawfully be exempted from subjection to ecclesiastical courts, we must and do affirm their exemption from them to be lawful. (VIII,9)

— *Faith* —

That which is true in itself and can neither be discerned by the senses nor deduced from merely natural principles must have been grounded in a revealed truth. In order to apprehend such truth we must have in us a habit of faith. The mysteries of our religion are beyond the reach of our understanding, beyond the reach of human reason, beyond all that any creature can comprehend. Therefore, the first thing required of one who seeks admission to Christ's family is belief, or faith. (V,63)

Faith consists not so much in knowledge as acknowledgement--acknowledgement of all things that heavenly wisdom reveals. (V,63)

The object of faith is above the reach of knowledge. Faith's love of God is beyond her comprehension of Him. (V,63)

This then is the foundation of our faith, upon which the frame of the Gospel is erected: it is that same Jesus whom the Virgin conceived by the Holy Ghost, whom Simon Peter embraced in his arms, whom Pilate condemned, whom the Jews crucified, whom the Apostles preached--the Lord, the only Savior of the world. We can lay down no other foundation but Him. (Discourse on Justification)

I know that I am not deceived and that I cannot deceive you when I teach the truth that the faith whereby you are saved cannot fail you. (Sermon on Certainty of Faith).

When we consider the things we believe to be true in and of themselves, it may be said that faith is more certain than science. (Sermon on Certainty of Faith).

Let the frailty of our nature, the subtlety of Satan, the force of our own deceivable imaginations all be as we know them to be--ready at every moment to threaten the utter subversion of our faith. Yet, faith is never really at risk. The prayer of Christ on our behalf is more than sufficient to strengthen us be we ever so weak, and to overthrow any power threatening us be it ever so strong and potent. (Sermon on Certainty of Faith)

Ours is a God who makes the most of what little faith we have, not a capricious sophister who gathers up the worst of our mistakes. (Discourse on Justification)

When the faith of a child of God is at its strongest, it is still weak; but even at its weakest, that faith is so strong that it will never fail completely--never perish--even in those who think it is extinguished within them. (Sermon on Certainty of Faith)

To be sure, our minds are so darkened with the foggy damp of original corruption that none of us has a heart so enlightened in knowledge or so firm in love of God's promise of salvation that his faith is perfect and free of doubt. (Sermon on Certainty of Faith)

By the "certainty of adherence," I mean that inclination of the heart to stick fast to what it believes.

This is a greater certainty for us than what we believe through reason because, as Christians, we know that God's laws and promises are not only true, they are also good. Therefore, even when the rational evidence of the truth of God's promises is so small that a person must grieve for the weakness of his faith in them, he still feels an adherence to them in his heart because he has at some time tasted the heavenly sweetness and the goodness of those promises. (Sermon on Certainty of Faith)

There is no doubt that our faith can operate secretly within us, unknown to us but known to God. (Sermon on Certainty of Faith)

I know in whom I have faith. I am not ignorant of whose precious blood was shed for me. I have a shepherd who is full of kindness, full of care, full of power. To Him I commit myself. (Sermon on Certainty of Faith)

To the end of my days I will labor to maintain the assurance of my faith, like a jewel. By a combination of my efforts and the gracious mediation of God's prayer I shall keep my faith. (Sermon on Certainty of Faith)

Even infidelity, extreme despair, hatred of God and all godliness, the stubbornness of sin, cannot prevail if there is the smallest spark of faith, love, hope or holiness left in us--just as the lowest degree of cold is not reached so long as there is one degree of heat remaining. (Discourse on Justification)

— *Fasting* —

Fasting has its origin in the laws of nature, is allowable in God's sight, has existed in all the ages before ours, and will probably be observed until the end of the world with singular usefulness and benefit. (V,72)

The use and practice of fasting, though less pleasant than feasting, is far more important because grief is a more familiar guest than the other passion, even though gladness is, naturally, more welcomed by everyone. Also, since the world is filled to overflowing with malice and so few people delight in doing good for others, everyone's woes are twice as many as his joys. Considering our corrupt inclinations, there was good reason for our Savior to count those happiest who mourned and for Solomon to judge it better to attend houses of mourning than places of feasting, not better in itself but better for relief of our common weakness. (V,72)

We hope that the poor, whose perpetual fasts are a necessity, may with greater contentment endure the hunger that virtue leads others to choose and, following the advice of the Church, to esteem hunger above its opposite. (V,72)

Since all evils cannot be rooted out, the most we can do is to try to keep them at a low ebb and create in the minds of people a love for a more frugal and disciplined life. This is the fruit we most look for in fasts, along with the undermining of palaces of depravity, the planting of frugality in natures once ruled by riotousness, the hardening of those melted by pleasure, and the healing of the tumor caused by gluttony. (V,72)

— *Fear* —

"Put them in fear, Oh God" say the Prophets, "so that they may know themselves to be but men, worms of the earth, dust and ashes, frail, corruptible, feeble things" (Psalms 9:20, 22:6; Job 25:6; Genesis 18:27). To shake off our false security and breed some healthy fear in the hearts of mortal men there are many admonitions about the power of evil, many threats of calamity, many descriptions of what is threatened. These are so lively that they leave an impression deep enough to keep our hearts continually awake. All of which demonstrates that we should fear nothing so much as…not being afraid. (Sermon on Remedy Against Fear and Sorrow)

The resurrection of the dead, the judgment of the world to come, and the endless misery of sinners, once apprehended, creates fear. … Fear is impotent and unable to direct itself, yet it has this benefit, namely, that people are thereby made to desire the prevention, if possible, of whatever evil they dread.… As fear of condemnation and disgrace among people, together with other civil punishments, are a bridle which restrains people from many heinous acts to which their outrage would lead, so the fear of divine revenge and punishment, when it occurs, makes human beings desire to be rid of that inward guilt of sin which they would otherwise continue to pursue. (VI,3)

It is nature that teaches the wise person to be fearful and hide himself; but it is grace and faith that teach him where to hide. Fools don't care where they hide their heads. But where shall the wise man hide when he fears the plague is coming? Where else should the frightened child hide but in the bosom of his loving father? Where should the Christian hide but under the shadow of the wings of Christ his Savior? (Sermon on Remedy Against Sorrow and Fear)

Because we are in danger like perused birds or like doves that seek but cannot find resting places that are right in front of them, our Savior has given us assurance so that fear would never overwhelm us and so that we would remember that, whatever evils may at any time beset us, we can always repair to Him for comfort, counsel, and help. (Sermon on Remedy Against Sorrow and Fear)

Fear is a good solicitor of devotion. Excessive fear grows out of apprehension of a God who has irresistible power to inflict pain. (V,3)

— *Forgiveness* —

Surely I must confess to you that if it be an error to think that God may be merciful to save us when we err, then my greatest comfort is my error. Were it not for the love I bear this error, I would neither wish to speak nor to live. (Discourse on Justification)

— *Free Will* —

Must the will cease to be itself because the will of God helps it? What is needed is a diligent and distinct consideration of what the human will possesses by nature, what it lacks through sin, and what it receives by means of grace. The capacity freely to accept or to refuse things set before it is so essential to the will that, were it deprived of this freedom, it would loose its nature and could not possibly retain the definition of will. (Dublin Fragments, IV)

Seeing that the natural freedom of a person's will was part of God's design in creating human beings (for this freedom is a part of human nature), the grace that was part of God's purpose in predestining human beings may and does perfect man but cannot possibly destroy his free will. God did not preordain the original sin that has wounded and overthrown the liberty that human beings originally had in their creation so that they could do good or evil. But God did foresee it, and predestined grace to serve as a remedy. Therefore, predestination for us also who are now sinful does not imply the bestowing of other natures than what people had at the beginning in creation, but the bestowing of gifts and the taking away of those impediments that have attached themselves to human nature through sin. (Dublin Fragments, IV)

Freedom of operation we have by nature; but the ability to live virtuously we have by grace. For through sin our nature has taken that disease and weakness whereby, left to itself, it inclines only to evil. Therefore, the natural powers and faculties of peoples' minds are, through our native corruption, so weakened and so adverse to God that, without the influence of His special grace, they bring forth nothing in His sight that is acceptable. Nevertheless, these powers and faculties of ours retain their natural manner of operation even though their original perfection is gone. People still have a reasonable understanding, and a will that is conformable to good things even though it is no longer able to direct itself to the good. Therefore, God has ordained grace to countervail our imbecility and to serve as His hand so that we, who cannot steer ourselves, may be drawn to the good. (Dublin Fragments, IV)

— *Freedom* —

Our opponents say that without some express commandment from God there is no power under heaven that may presume by any decree to limit the freedom that God has given us. This opinion shakes the fabric of human government, produces anarchy and utter confusion, dissolves families, weakens colleges, corporations, and armies, overthrows kingdoms, churches, and whatever is currently upheld by the providence of God or human authority and power. (V,71)

The rules of men cannot possibly work without some abridgement of the liberty of those to whom they are applied. (V,71)

Obedience accompanied by openly expressed unwillingness to obey is no better than open disobedience. (V,29)

Those actions that the law of God leaves arbitrary and therefore free for us to decide are nevertheless subject to human laws that abridge individual freedom for the common good, insofar as the rules of equity apply. We must either maintain this limitation on individual liberty or else see the world overturned as each person becomes a law unto himself. (V,71)

— *Funerals (Burials)* —

The purpose of funeral obligations is, first, to show a natural love toward the deceased person, then to show the honor appropriate to all people generally and to the deceased in particular, and, finally, to testify to the responsibility that the Church has to comfort the living and to proclaim the hope that we all have concerning the resurrection of the dead. (V,75)

Just as mourning at such times is appropriate, so is it suitable to wear a certain kind of clothing to show a sorrowful affection. White garments are suitable to wear at marriage feasts and other times of joy. Why is not the opposite apparel just as suitable in times of grief as white is in times of joy? (V,75)

There is no doubt that the desire of the people both to live and to die well is increased when they know that their death will not be folded up in silence but that the ears of many will hear of their departure. Furthermore, when they hear how mercifully God has dealt with their brethren in their final hours, in addition to the praise they give to God and the joy that they have--or should have--because of their fellowship with the saints, is not their hope much confirmed about their own death? (V,75)

The greatest thing about the duty to provide a Christian burial is the outward testimony to the hope that we have for the resurrection of the dead. Let anyone of good judgment decide whether it is better for a company of people to bring a corpse in silent procession to the burial site and then leave it there to be covered with dirt, and that is the end of it, or to have a funeral service devoutly performed with a solemn recital of such lectures, Psalms, and prayers as have been designed to stir up people's minds to a careful consideration of their situation both here on earth and afterwards. (V,75)

Has it ever at any time before now been heard that either the Church or any Christian person of sound belief has judged funeral services to be inappropriate, indecent, or unfit? Only in these miserable days of ours are the most effective means to testify and to strengthen true religion plucked at and, in some instances, pulled up by their very roots under the guise of removing supposedly superstitious abuses in our Church. By all means take away this practice that the Church has ordained to offer the hope of God for the dead! But in those silent funerals that are espoused by our critics what single thing is there left whereby the world may know that we are Christians? (V,75)

— *God* —

God has true immutability and eternity, that is to say, a continuance within which no variety or addition develops from the beginning of time until now. (V,69)

From God all things received their original being and their continuation as the things that they are. In this sense, everything partakes of God, is His offspring, and bears the marks of His influence. (V,56)

The glory of all things resides in that wherein their highest perfection consists. (V,42)

God requires the most sincere affection to Him that can be yielded by the force of our minds and souls. If we regard Him as any less than far above all other things, our religion lacks the inner perfection that it should have and we do not worship Him as our God. (V,6)

It is impossible for God to withdraw His presence from anything because He is infinite by nature. He fills heaven and earth, although He takes up no room in either because His substance is immaterial, pure, and, to us, incomprehensible. Although no part of us is ever absent from God, who is present in every particular thing, yet we do not see His presence within us. Partly by reason and more completely by faith, we know firmly and certainly that God is present in us. This divine presence is the consequence of an infinite and incomprehensible substance. For, what can be everywhere, yet nowhere seen? (V,55)

God knows better than we do the best times and the best means and the best things to give us for the good of our souls. (Sermon on Matthew 7.7)

If the name "Lord" does not seem sufficiently full of grace for you, then surely the Holy Spirit has given you courage to call upon God with a cheerful voice like children calling their Father. Enlarge your hearts and there is no good thing you can desire that your Father's indulgence does not invite you to expect from Him. …. It is not with God as it is with human beings whose titles show what they should be rather than what they are. God will not be called what He is not. His name reveals His nature. If His affection were not fatherly the name Father would offend Him. Fathers lay up treasures for their children. (Sermon on Pride/Justice)

Is it up to us to understand how God brings His words and purposes about?… Let it always content us to take His word as an absolute promise that we shall receive and find what we seek in the end. "It shall be opened unto you." How? Where? By what means? Leave all that up to God. (Sermon on Matthew 7.7)

Our very virtues may be snares to entrap us. The enemy that waits for any occasion to work our ruin has always found it harder to overthrow a humble sinner than a proud saint. There is no one's position so dangerous as his whom Satan has persuaded that his own righteousness shall present him pure and blameless in the sight of God. (Discourse on Justification)

It is the glory of God to give. His very nature delights in it. His mercy, flowing in the current through which we all pass, may seem dried up along the way but at the end it never fails. (Sermon on Matthew 7.7)

He that promises half his kingdom foresees that when that is gone the remainder is only half of what it was. What we give we lose. But what God bestows benefits us and takes nothing from Him. There are no fearful restraints in His offers. (Sermon on Matthew 7.7)

— *Godparents* —

Out of tender mercy for children, God allows the professions of faith and promises made for them in Baptism by godparents to be of no less effect than if they had been able to make them on their own. No one is more fit to undertake this office on their behalf than those godparents who present them for Baptism. (V,64)

— *Grace* —

There are three kinds of grace: the grace whereby God inclines towards human beings, the grace of outward instruction, and the grace of inward sanctification. The first two cause the human inclination towards God, for the first is the wellspring of all good, and the second the instrument that leads us to our good. The third, which effectively causes the first two in us who have no reason whatsoever to think ourselves worthy of either, is the gracious and blessed gift of His Holy Spirit. (Dublin Fragments, Vol. IV, p. 112)

God's grace, poured into His people, assures us that, despite all of our sin and all of our doubting, we will never be separated from His love or cut off from Christ Jesus. The seed of God abides forever in His children and shields them from any irremediable wound. (Sermon on Certainty of Faith)

— *Heaven* —

The life in God begun here will be finished in the world to come. (Sermon on Pride)

Happy, therefore, are those who, whatever misery may befall them in this world, are secure in a certain expectation of what God has promised: happiness and true life in the world to come. (Sermon on Pride)

— *Heresy* —

There are only **four ingredients** that combine to make up the whole of our Lord Jesus Christ: His divinity, His manhood, the combination of these two, and the distinction that remained between the two when they were joined. There are **four major heresies** that have stood against these four truths: first, the Arians, by arguing against the divinity of Christ; secondly, the Apollinarians, by distorting and misinterpreting that which belongs to His human nature; thirdly, the Nestorians, by rending Christ asunder and dividing Him into two persons; fourthly, the Eutychians, by confounding in His person the two natures that they should have distinguished. Against these four heresies there have been **four Councils** of the ancient Church: the Council of Nicea, to defend the Church from the Arians; the Council of Constantinople, against the Apollinarians; the Council of Ephesus, against the Nestorians; The Council of Chalcedon, against the Eutychians. (V,54)

People separate themselves from the Church in several ways: heresy, schism, and apostasy. If they loose the ties of faith by openly opposing any principal point of Christian doctrine, they have separated themselves by heresy. If they break the bonds of unity that hold together the body of the Church by willfully forsaking the holy, pure, and orderly exercises established in the Church, they have separated themselves by schism. If they willfully cast off and forsake both profession of Christ and communion with Christians and take leave of all religion, they have separated themselves by apostasy. (First Sermon on Jude)

Heretics, where they err on points of doctrine, have forsaken the true Church of God. (V,68)

The weeds of heresy grown to such ripeness will, even in their cutting down, often scatter the seeds which, lying for a time unseen and buried in the earth, will later spring up freshly and be no less pernicious than at the first. (V,42)

We must make a distinction between those who stray from God out of ignorance of the truth but retain a mind desirous of being instructed and those who persist in stubborn defense of their blindness even after the truth is laid open to them. (Discourse on Justification)

Some heresies concern matters of belief, such as transubstantiation of sacramental elements in the

Eucharist. Others concern matters of practice, such as adoration of the elements. It is important to note that sometimes the practice is followed without any belief in the supporting doctrine. (Discourse on Justification)

The question is not whether an error is made but whether that mistake excludes the possibility of salvation unless it is expressly recanted or repented of. For my part, I dare not deny the possibility of salvation for Lutherans when they have been the chief instrument of our own redemption, even if they do carry to their graves a doctrine [Nestorian heresy] that is greatly repugnant to the truth. (Discourse on Justification)

Evil ministers of good things are like torches, a light to others and a waste to none but themselves. (V,62)

—— *Holy (Festival) Days* ——

There is no doubt that, just as God's extraordinary presence has hallowed and sanctified certain places, so His extraordinary works, which have truly and worthily advanced certain times, ought to lead all people who honor God to regard those dates as holier than others. (V,69)

The sanctification of days and times is a token of that thankfulness and a part of that public honor that we owe God for His admirable benefits. It is not sufficient that we keep a private calendar for these benefits and, as we see fit, take our separate individual occasions to thank God for all that He had done for mankind. The days that are chosen to serve as public memorials of His mercies should be clothed with the outer robes of holiness so that their difference from other days is made clear. (V,70)

If what befalls us makes us glad, our festival celebrations declare our joy to be in Him whose undeserved mercy is the author of all happiness. If we want to avoid anything that is either immanent or present, then our watchings, fastings, cries, and tears are all honest testimonials that we blame ourselves as the sole cause of our own misery and acknowledge God as no less likely than He is able to save us. (V,72)

The most natural testimonies of our joy on these special days are first, to sing God's praises with a cheerful lightness of mind, secondly, to express our pleasure and delight by generous giving beyond our usual contributions, and thirdly, to cease our ordinary labor, the toils and cares of which are not suitable companions of our gladness. Festival ceremony is, therefore, nothing but a proper mixture of praise, charitable giving, and peaceful rest. (V,70)

Religious festivals, whether ordained by God Himself or by his Church under authority given by God, are public religious services that should be used periodically. This periodic repetition is an effective way to bring to full maturity and growth those seeds of godliness that even our critics grant are sown in the hearts of many thousands of people during these festival holy days. (V,70)

God in His wisdom has especially commended one feature of holy festival days, that they provide children and newcomers their first occasion to ask about and seek God. If even this much goodness results from our festivals, let the Church learn to pray to God that he preserve them. (V,71)

To celebrate these sacred religious days well is to spend the flower of our time happily. These days are the splendor and outward dignity of our religion; they are powerful witness to an ancient truth; they are provocations to the exercise of our faith; they are shadows of eternal happiness in heaven; they are, on earth, everlasting records and memorials. (V,71)

—— *Human Nature* ——

If no natural or accidental incapacity inhibits the desire to do good, people always delight in doing what benefits others. (V,1)

Even as all creatures that attain their highest perfection in the fullness of time are at their beginning raw, so man, who is closest to perfection when at the end of his race, is at the entrance to life so weak that he is forced to depend on the voluntary good will of those who have no reason to help him except the secret inclination to repay to the common stock of humanity the help they once needed and borrowed. In this the condition of all humanity is the same. (Sermon on Matthew 7.7)

Such is the perverse constitution of our nature that we neither understand perfectly the way of the Lord, nor steadfastly embrace it when it is understood, nor graciously utter it when it is embraced, nor peaceably maintain it when it is preached. The best of us is overtaken sometimes by blindness, sometimes by impatience, sometimes by other passions of the mind to which, as God knows, we are subject. (Discourse on Justification)

There are those who commend very highly the felicity of the supposedly innocent world, in which they claim that human beings embraced faithfulness and honesty of their own accord, not out of fear of the magistrate or of retribution staring them in the face if they did otherwise. There are those who affirm that what holds people in check is the shame of wrongdoing and that the love of fairness and justice is itself a bar against great abuses of power. There are those who describe for us states of natural happiness and never mention religion. But all of these people are declaring what is in truth the singular handiwork of religion. If religion sincerely and sufficiently possessed the hearts of all people, not other restraint from evil doing would be needed. (V,1)

What creature is more savage, wilder, and more cruel than the person who sees himself able, either by fraud to overreach or by power to break, the laws to which he should be subject? Given such great boldness to cause offence, it is necessary that people be held in check, not by vain hope but by a full awareness on their part of something they are powerless to withstand. This is what we mean by the political use of religion. (V,2)

In a word, it is not the person on whom no calamity falls, but he whom neither misery nor prosperity is able to move from the right course, whom we may truly pronounce fortunate. What ever misfortune happens outwardly to such people in this life, unless is has appeared in the eyes of sound and impartial judges to have resulted from divine revenge for previous wrongdoing, should be regarded as but an example of the common human tragedy to which we are all subject. No misery should be reckoned as anything more than the common human lot, once God has determined that we will pass through it and come safely to the other shore. (V,76)

— *Humility* —

Humility is a proper virtue in supplicants. To testify to our humility by strong affirmation of our unworthiness reveals a sound grasp of the supreme glory and majesty of the One before whom we stand and it places in His hands a kind of pledge or bond against our ingratitude, the natural cause of which is always either ignorance, dissimulation or pride. (V,47)

The patience and meekness of Christ in putting up with injuries done to Him is worthy of our imitation. His humility ought to be sufficient to humble us no matter how grievous and insufferable the wrongs done to us may seem. (Sermon on Pride/Justice)

— *Idolatry* —

Idolaters are miserable in two ways. In the first place, they find no succor in that which they worship; and secondly, from the hands of the One they should worship they can expect only the fruits of His justifiable displeasure: the withdrawing of His grace, abandonment in this world, and confusion in the world to come. (V,17)

We should abhor whatever idolaters may have thought or done that is idolatrous but not everything they have ever thought or done; for God is the author of the good that often resides within evil. (V,12)

— *Incarnation* —

We lack the ability to express perfectly--or even to conceive--the manner in which the Incarnation happened. The strength of our faith is tested by those things wherein our minds and imaginations are not strong. Nevertheless, because this divine mystery is more true than understandable, many have bent the truth to suit their opinions and fancies so that we find in their expositions more of explanation than of truth. In the space of fifteen hundred years since Christ, the Church has been troubled with nothing so much as the work of preserving this article of faith [the Incarnation] from the sinister constructions of heretics. (V,52)

If we need a reason why the Son rather than the Father or the Holy Ghost was made man, we should ask ourselves whether we who are born of the children of wrath could be adopted as God's children in any other way than by God's natural Son serving as the mediator between God and us. (V,51)

Christ is a Person who is both divine and human at the same time. He is not two persons within one but a divine Person who is personally the Son of God. He is human in that He really has the nature of the children of men. In Christ there is, therefore, a twofold substance, not a twofold person, because one person would extinguish the other whereas one nature cannot be nullified by another. (V,52)

The Son of God did not take a man's person unto Himself but a man's nature unto His own pre-existent divine Person. Thus He took the semen--the seed of Abraham--the very first element of our nature before it had developed any personal substance. The flesh and its conjunction with God happened in an instant. Christ's creation and His taking unto Himself our flesh was a single act. So in Christ there is only one Person, from everlasting to everlasting. In taking on the nature of a man, He remained one Person and did not change anything but the form of His nature. (V,52)

The cause of the spiritual life in us is Christ, not as He inhabits us in some carnal or bodily sense, but as something dwelling in our souls which, when the mind apprehends it, is said to inhabit and possess the mind. (Discourse on Justification)

If it is asked what the Person of the Son of God acquired by assuming manhood, surely the whole sum of it is that He was then capable of lesser deeds than His Person would otherwise have allowed. The only gain He purchased for Himself was to be capable of loss and injury for the sake of others. (V,54)

Does anyone really doubt that from the flesh of Christ our bodies receive that life that will make them glorious and that they are already part of His blessed body? Our corruptible bodies could never live the lives they shall one day live were it not that right here and now they are joined to His incorruptible body. That His body is in ours is the cause of our immortality because, through His death and merit, He has removed the cause of our mortality. Christ is, therefore, both as God and as man, that true vine of which we are branches, both spiritually and physically. (V,56)

Just as Christ does not dwell in everyone, so He does not work equally in all of us within whom He does dwell. So it appears that the participation of Christ, which derives from both His divine and human nature, operates in us in varying degrees and with differing effects. But these effects are, nevertheless, really operating within us and we may truly be said to possess Him. Christ imparts

Himself to us and inhabits us with more or less portion and greater or smaller degrees of His grace as it flows into us from Him. (V,56)

— *Indifferent (Unnecessary) Matters* —

The Apostle Paul says, "All things are lawful for me" (1 Cor. 6:12), speaking, as it seems, in the person of the Christian gentile for maintenance of our liberty in matters that are indifferent [unnecessary]. Nevertheless, his answer is that "All things are not necessary." In things indifferent there is a choice; they are not always equally necessary. (II,4)

It is not that **we** make some things *necessary* and some things *accessory* and secondary. Our Lord and Savior Himself made that distinction when he declared such things as mercy and faith to be *greater and weightier* than other matters. (III,3)

By what construction is anyone alive able to make that distinction untrue that separates things of external governance and ceremony [indifferent matters] in the Church from things necessary to salvation? (III,3)

The wearing of vestments is only an indifferent matter authorized in our laws because the wisdom of our church authorities has deemed it appropriate to do so. (V,29)

When God flatly commands us to abstain from things [wearing certain vestments] that are in themselves indifferent but which offend our weaker brethren, His meaning is that we should obey this kind of commandment only if we can do so without abandoning that which He has absolutely commanded in a matter [preaching] that is not indifferent. (V, 29)

From those who trouble us with such doubts we would like to be resolved of a greater doubt, namely, whether it is not a way of taking God's name in vain to debase religion with such frivolous disputes, a sin to bestow time and effort over such matters. These are [indifferent] matters of such small importance and quality …that they become distasteful when they are disputed. (V, 30)

I mean by "tradition" those ordinances made in the earliest days of the Christian religion, established by the authority that Christ had bestowed on his Church in matters indifferent to be observed until the Church finds reasonable cause to change them. (V, 65)

— *Judging* —

We must beware not to sit as little gods in judgement of others and, as mere opinion or fancy leads us, rashly to decide if this person is sincere or that person a hypocrite. … Who are you to take it upon yourselves to judge another? Judge yourself! God has given us infallible evidence whereby we may at any time give true and righteous sentence upon ourselves. We cannot examine the hearts of others. We may, however, examine our own hearts. (First Sermon on Jude)

— *Jurisdiction* —

Besides that spiritual power, which is instituted in order to require the performance of those [pastoral] duties which have already been sufficiently discussed, there is in the Church a second kind of authority, no less necessary, which we call the power of jurisdiction. (VI,2)

Jurisdiction is power to command and judge according to law. Spiritual jurisdiction is a power of commanding and judging in spiritual affairs according to spiritual laws. Those who have power to command and judge must also have authority to punish. (Autograph Notes, p. 466)

I conclude that spiritual authority is a power that Christ has given to be used over those who are subject to it for the eternal good of their souls, according to His own most sacred laws and the wholesome positive ordinances of the Church. (VI,2)

None have ordinary power to chastise souls except those [the order of the priesthood] to whom the charge and care of souls is committed. (Autograph Notes, p. 469)

The spiritual power of the Church is such that it cannot be challenged by natural right or instituted by human authority, for its forces and effects are supernatural and divine. … Christ gave this power to the Church for the benefit and good of souls, as a means for keeping them on the path that leads to endless happiness, and as a bridle to hold them within their due and convenient bounds, and, if they do go astray, as a forcible help to reclaim them. (VI,1)

God alone forgives sin; He alone cleanses the soul from inward blemish, and looses the debt of eternal death. He has not given to His priests such a great privilege; nevertheless, He has authorized His priests to loose and bind, that is to say, to declare who are bound and who are forgiven. For even if a person is already cleared before God, he or she is not cleared in the face of the Church other than by the priest's sentence, who likewise may be said to bind by imposing requirements and satisfactions and to loose by admitting to Holy Communion. (VI,6)

— *Justice* —

God is the author, the fountain, and the cause of our justice. (Sermon on Pride/Justice)

Justice always implies these things: first, that there is some good thing that is due from one person to another; secondly, that there is a law, either natural or positive, that makes this an obligation; thirdly, that the person who has the obligation does what the law commands. (Sermon on Pride/Justice)

Justice can be defined as that virtue that assures that we have what we need in the manner prescribed by law. Neither God nor angels nor man may in any sense be called just except by reference to some law of justice that operates among them. (Sermon on Pride/Justice)

Justice is that virtue whereby the good, which we lack, is received, inoffensively, from the hands of others. (Sermon on Pride/Justice)

Justice is that virtue wherein we receive good things in such manner and degree as the law prescribes. (Sermon on Pride/Justice)

There is no injustice unless a wrong is willfully committed. (Sermon on Pride/Justice)

So natural is the union of religion with justice that we may boldly deny that there is either where both are not. How can they be unfeignedly just whom religion does not cause to be so, or how can they be religious who are not found to be so by the justice of their actions? (V,1)

Justice is that whereby the poor have their help, the rich their ease, the powerful their honor, the souls of the departed their endless rest and peace. Justice is that by which God and angels and men are exalted. Justice is the primary matter in contention today in the Christian world. In a word, justice is that wherein not only our present happiness but also our future joy in the kingdom of God depends. Whether we are in love with one another, with things present, or things to come, we need to be instructed by justice. (Sermon on Pride/Justice)

The wrong that people do God for lack of a right understanding of the workings of His justice is nowhere clearer than in the complaints about the hard and heavy calamities of the righteous and the arrogant prosperity of the godless. … Our universally agreed upon sense of justice is that imprisonments, banishments, restraint of liberty, deprivation of rank, diminution of possessions, loss of life and limb, in fact anything penal and unpleasant, is to be meted out only to dangerous and deadly criminals. So that when the Supreme Guide and Governor of heaven takes a completely contrary course of action, depressing and in every way keeping down the good and virtuous while crowning the heads of malignants with honor and heaping happiness upon them, this can hardly seem to us to be just or righteous on His part. (Sermon on Pride/Justice)

— *Justification* —

The righteousness wherein we must be found if we are to be justified is not our own. Therefore, we cannot be justified by any inherent quality. Christ alone merited righteousness for Himself and for as many as are "found in Him". In Christ, God finds us if we are faithful for by faith alone we are incorporated into Him. Then, although in ourselves we are altogether sinful and unrighteous, being found in Christ, no matter how impious and full of iniquity and sin we are, through faith and repentance we are seen by God with a gracious eye and accepted, pardoned, and made righteous in Christ as though we had never sinned at all. In the sight of God we are perfectly righteous in Christ as though we had fulfilled all of His commandments. (Discourse on Justification)

Unless there is some ambiguity in these words [salvation, righteousness, justification and sanctification], St. Paul and St. James seem to contradict one another on the issue of faith and works. This cannot be. What we discover is that justification for Paul does not imply sanctification when he says that we are justified by faith without works. Justification does sometimes imply sanctification for St. James. So there are two kinds of righteousness, one which is imputed to us by God and one which consists of our works of faith, hope, charity and other Christian virtues. (Discourse on Justification)

If you demand to know which of these two kinds of justification we received first, I answer that it is the habitual justice that is first engrafted in or imputed to us. Actual righteousness, which comes through good works, comes afterwards both in order of importance and in time. When we attentively study this matter we see clearly that the faith of true believers cannot be divorced from love and hope, that faith is a part of sanctification, that faith is perfected by good works, and that no work of ours is good without faith. (Discourse on Justification)

The results of this sanctifying righteousness are the fruits and the operations [works] of the faithful spirit. The distinction here is between *habitual* and *actual* righteousness. *Habitual* is that with which souls are inwardly endowed from the time when we first become the temples of the Holy Ghost. *Actual* is that holiness for which Enoch, Job, Zachary, Elizabeth, and other Saints in Scripture are so highly commended. (Discourse on Justification)

── *Kings* ──

The power of dominion is supreme authority. … He is called supreme who has neither superior nor colleague in authority. … Law is the command of the supreme power.... The crown of England is imperial in itself and has no superior but God. (Autograph Notes, III)

Where the law gives dominion, who doubts that the king who receives it must receive and hold it according to that old axiom: "The king attributes to the law what the law attributes to him: power and dominion." And again: "A king ought not to be under other people, but only under God and the law." (VIII,1)

When Christian kings are said to have spiritual dominion or supreme power in ecclesiastical affairs and causes, the meaning is that within their own precincts and territories they have authority and power to command even in matters of Christian religion and that there is no one higher or greater who can countermand them in those cases where they are placed to reign as kings. (VIII,2)

The greatest reason we have to be happy for some Christian kings and admire them above other kings is not because of their long reigns, their calm and quiet departure from this life, the settled establishment of the succession from their own flesh, the glorious overthrow of foreign enemies, or the wise prevention of dangers and conspiracies at home. In truth the reason we extol the happiness of some kings is that, if it is true that they have ruled virtuously, if honors paid to them have not filled their hearts with pride, if they have exercised their power in the service of and attendance upon the majesty of the Most High, if they have feared God as their own subjects and inferiors have feared them, if they have loved neither pomp nor pleasure more than heaven, if revenge has come slowly from them and mercy has been offered willingly, if they have so tempered harshness with leniency that extreme severity does not cut off those in whom there is hope of amendment of life and shown ease of pardoning offences that does not embolden offenders, if, knowing that whatever they do their use of power should demonstrate that they have been careful not to do anything but what is commendable in the best of men and not simply in great personages, if the true knowledge of themselves has humbled them in God's sight no less than God has raised them up in the eyes of men, then, I say, we may reckon them to be the happiest among the mightiest in the world. (V,76)

The best and most renowned prelates of the Church of Christ have endured the wrath of kings here on earth rather than yield to the harsh desires of these princes who, following poor advice and counsel, have coveted that which they should have left God alone to enjoy. There are martyrs whom posterity much honors for inventing ways to conceal from kings the church treasures in their custody even as they gladly neglected the safety of their own lives. (V,79)

— *Knowledge (See Also Reason)* —

In the matter of knowledge, there is this difference between the angels of God and human children. Angels already have full and complete knowledge in the highest degree that can be imparted to them; humans, if we view them at their beginning, are at first without understanding or knowledge of any kind. Nevertheless, from this utter vacuity they grow by degrees, until they come at length to be even as the angels themselves. (I, 6)

Therefore, since the soul of a human person is in the beginning like a book wherein nothing is written and yet upon which all things may be imprinted, we shall now search out by what steps and degrees it rises to perfection as knowledge. …. The human soul, being capable of a more divine perfection, has, besides the faculties of growing in sensible knowledge which is common to us and beasts, a further ability that the beasts do not share with us, namely, the ability to reach higher than for mere knowledge of the senses. But until we grow to some ripeness of years, the human soul only fills itself with concepts of an inferior and more accessible nature which may later serve as instruments for attaining a higher level of understanding. In the meantime, the human soul does not attain any knowledge that is higher than the understanding of lesser creatures. When it once comprehends anything beyond this level (such as differences in time, affirmations, negations, and contradictions in speech), we then recognize it as involving some use of reason. ... Afterwards there might be added the full assistance of true art and learning. ... [These are] education and instruction which are both instruments- -the first by example and the second by precept--that enable our natural faculty of reason to more quickly and accurately distinguish between truth and error, good and evil. (I, 6)

The main principles of reason are in themselves apparent. For, not to make anything self evident to human understanding would be to take away all possibility of knowing anything.... In every kind of knowledge there are some such grounds that, once being proposed, the mind immediately embraces them as free from all possibility of error, clear and manifest without proof. An axiom or principle of this more general kind is: the greater good is chosen before the lesser good. ... Less general axioms that are still so manifest that they need no further proof or discourse include: "God is to be worshiped"; "Parents are to be honored"; "Others are to be treated by us as we ourselves would be treated by them." As soon as such things are alleged, all people acknowledge them to be good. (I,8)

There is a kind of knowledge that God has always revealed to us in the works of nature. Although this sort of wisdom has long been honored and highly esteemed as being profound, it does not save us. That which saves believers is knowledge of the Cross of Christ. (V,22)

We do not bring knowledge of God with us into the world. No one ever believes in God unless the doctrines of faith are instilled in him by the instruction of others. (V,21)

God, in His incomprehensible wisdom, has decided to limit the visible effects of His power--and hence our knowledge of Him--to the extent that seems best to Him. Therefore He provides us with certainty in all that we need to know for salvation in the life to come. But He does not give us certain knowledge of how to achieve perfection in this life. (Sermon on Certainty of Faith)

"Truth," they say, "is the daughter of time." And who doubts that in time God will make clear that which we do not now understand? Must we deny that which we do not perfectly understand? (Sermon on Pride/Justice)

It is a lack of knowledge of God that causes all the wrong-doing among people just as it is the knowledge of God that is the sure ground of all our happiness and the seed of whatever perfect virtue might grow in us. (V,18)

General principles, especially in matters of civic and church affairs, cast a cloudy mist before the eye of our common sense because we can never fully discern the many exceptions that lie hidden within them. Those who walk in darkness do not know where they are going and those who are guided by principles alone can be no more certain of their direction. Unqualified generalities are popular with the public because they seem so simple at first sight. They are less obvious to people of good judgment because these absolute principles cannot safely be trusted to be applicable to particular cases. (V,9)

— *Law* —

Of law there can be no less acknowledged than that her seat is the bosom of God, her voice the harmony of the world. All things in heaven and earth do her homage, the very least feeling her care, the greatest not exempted from her power. (I,16)

The eye of the law is the eye of God. The law looks into the hearts and inner dispositions of people and beholds how much one star differs from another. (V,81)

God's laws are the sacred image of His wisdom. He will punish severely those blatant or subtle crimes that would rarely be tried in the courts of human justice. (V,81)

A law, in the general sense, is a rule directed to goodness of operation.… The rule of voluntary agents on earth is the sentence that reason gives concerning the goodness of those things that we are supposed to do. (I,8)

We define a law as that which assigns to each thing the **kind**, that which moderates the **force and power**, that which appoints the **form and measure** of its working. (I,2)

We must remember that we should claim nothing on our own behalf or that of others unless there is warrant for doing so in the law and unless the judgment is handed down by at least two persons other than ourselves. (Sermon on Pride/Justice)

Whenever two laws, through an unintended result, contradict one another in such a way that both cannot be followed, there is nothing for it but to obey that law which will do the least harm to the public good. (Sermon on Pride/Justice)

It is not simply what people seek under law, but what they seek that is reasonable and does not produce contradictions in the law, that is lawful. (Sermon on Pride/Justice)

Students of public policy have taught consistently that commonwealths are founded upon laws and that only by a general acceptance of these laws, which keep them in order, can a people be formed into a single body politic. (Discourse on Justification)

The ground of all civil law is this: *No one ought to be hurt or injured by another.* Take away this agreement and you take away all laws; take away all laws and what becomes of commonwealths? (Discourse on Justification)

Thus we see how one and the same thing is under diverse considerations conveyed through many laws, and that to measure by any one kind of law all the actions of humans is to confound the admirable order in which God has disposed all laws, each in itself distinct in its nature and degree. Hence, no less can be acknowledged concerning law than that her seat is the bosom of God, her voice the harmony of the world. All things in heaven and earth do her homage: the very least as feeling her care, and the greatest as not exempted from her power. But angels and humans and creatures of whatever condition, though each in a different way and manner, yet all with uniform consent, admire her as the mother of their peace and joy. (I,16)

— *Types Of Law* —

That law which is laid in the bosom of God we call <u>eternal</u>. This law receives different and various names according to the different kinds of things which are subject to it. That part of eternal law which orders natural agents we usually call <u>nature's law</u>. That part of eternal law which angels clearly behold and obey without any swerving is a <u>celestial and heavenly law</u>. The <u>law of</u> <u>reason</u> is that which binds reasonable creatures in this world, and by reason they may most plainly perceive themselves to be bound by it. <u>Divine law</u> binds reasonable creatures in this world but is not known except by special revelation from God. <u>Human law</u>, whether derived by reason or from God, when judged to be probably expedient, is made a law. All things therefore, which are as they ought to be, are conformed according to this <u>second eternal law</u>, and even those things which are not conformable to this eternal law are, notwithstanding, in some way ordered by the <u>first eternal law</u>. For what good or evil is there under the sun, what action corresponding or repugnant to the law that God has imposed upon his creatures, except that God works in or upon it according to the law which He has eternally purposed to keep, that is, the <u>first eternal law</u>? (I,3)

<u>Eternal Law</u>: Such operations as have their beginning and being by a voluntary purpose whereby God has eternally decreed when and how they should be, we call eternal law. (I,2)

We may therefore designate as eternal law that order which God before all ages has set down for Himself to do all things by. (I.,2)

Natural/Physical Law: We sometimes mean by this phrase "natural law" that manner of working which God has set for each created thing to follow. This law applies to those things which keep the law of their kind unwittingly and are therefore most properly called "natural" agents, such as the heavens and elements of the world which can do no otherwise than they do. We give intellectual natures the name of "voluntary" agents so that we may distinguish them from the other. It is expedient that we separate the law of nature observed by the one from that to which the other is tied. (I,3)

Law of Reason: Where understanding is lacking, reason is the director of a person's will by discovering in behavior that which is good. For the laws of well doing are the dictates of right reason. (I,8)

People commonly used to call rational law the <u>law of nature</u>, meaning thereby the law to which human nature, by reason, knows itself to be universally bound; for this reason, it is more fitly termed the <u>law of reason</u>. This law, I say, comprehends all those things which people evidently know, or at least may know, by the light of their natural understanding to be proper or improper, virtuous or vicious, good or evil for them to do. (I,8)

The light of natural understanding, wit, and reason is from God. He it is who thereby illuminates every human being entering into the world. If anything proceeds from us that is corrupt and useless, the mother thereof is our own ignorance; neither does it proceed from any such cause whereof God is the author. He is the author of all that we think or do by virtue of that light which He Himself has given. Therefore, the laws which the heathen drew up to direct their actions, insofar as they proceeded from the light of nature, God acknowledges to have proceeded from Himself, and that He was the writer of them in the tables of their hearts. (III,9)

<u>Political or Human Law</u>: Political laws, ordained for external order and rule among people, are never framed as they should be unless we understand that people are inwardly willful, obstinate, rebellious and averse to obeying the sacred laws of their own nature. In a word, we must assume that people in their depraved minds are little better than wild beasts and thus our laws must so order their outward actions that they cannot hinder the common welfare for which human societies are instituted. Unless our laws do this they are imperfect. (I,10)

The first kind of thing addressed by human law is whatever in itself is either naturally good or evil. These matters may be too subtle for the discernment of most people without further explanation and judgment. And, since there are so many different ways to err, many people would remain ignorant of their duties unless such matters were set forth in laws. (I,10)

Those who are learned in the laws of this land observe that our statutes sometimes are only the affirmation or ratification of that which by common law was previously obeyed. Generally speaking, all human laws that are made for the ordering of political societies are either such as establish some duty to which all persons earlier stood bound by the law of reason or else such as make that a duty which before was not. The first kind we may, for clarity's sake, call "mixed," and the other "merely" human law. ... We call a law "mixed" because the matter to which it binds is the same which reason requires of us; it differs from the law of reason only in the manner in which it binds us. For whereas people before stood bound in conscience to do as the law of reason teaches, they have now, by virtue of human law, become constrainable and punishable if they outwardly transgress. As for laws that are "merely" human, their subject is anything that reason teaches as probably fit and convenient. But, until such time as such a law has been legislated, it binds no individual person. (I,10)

Law may be natural, and therefore immutable, or else a law may be subject to change--which we call "positive law." The failure to distinguish between these two types of law has obscured the meaning of justice more than a little. (Sermon on Pride/Justice)

[There is a] misconception that all laws that men establish are "positive" and so changeable, and all laws that God establishes are immutable. Not so. It is not the author but the object of law that defines the distinction. They also differ in this way: a positive (changeable) law is one that binds those to whom it applies in those things that might previously have been done or not done without offence. But the rule applies for only so long as the law is in force. … On the other hand there is no person and no time for which an unchangeable law of nature is not binding. If, for example, God had never spoken a word to us concerning the duty that children owe to their parents, yet from the first-born of Adam until the very last of us, *Honor thy father and mother* would have bound us all. (Sermon on Pride/Justice)

Human laws must be made according to the general laws of nature, and without contradicting any positive law in Scripture. Otherwise they are ill made. With regard to [human positive] laws made and received by a whole Church, those people who live within the bosom of the Church must not think it an indifferent matter whether or not they obey them. (III,9)

<u>International Law</u>.   Besides that law which simply concerns people as people, and that law which belongs to those who are linked with others in some form of political society, there is a third kind of law which touches all political bodies insofar as one of them has public commerce with another. This third kind of law is the <u>law of nations</u>.… The national laws of mutual commerce between societies in former and better times might have been different from today when nations are so prone to offer violence, injury, and wrong doing. Hence, there has emerged a distinction in all three kinds of law between <u>primary</u> and <u>secondary</u> law. The former is grounded upon virtuous human nature, the other is built upon depraved nature. <u>Primary</u> laws of nations are either those concerning embassy, such as the courteous entertainment of foreigners and strangers, or they serve to regulate extensive traffic between nations, and the like. <u>Secondary</u> laws of nations are the kind that this unquiet world are most familiar and acquainted with: I mean laws of war, which are better known than kept. (I,10)

The strength and virtue of the law of nations is such that no particular nation can lawfully override them by any of its several laws and ordinances, any more than an individual can negate by private resolutions the law of the whole commonwealth or state in which that person lives. For just as civil law, being the act of a whole political body, overrules each individual part of that same body, so there is no reason that any one commonwealth of itself should, to the prejudice of another, annihilate that whereupon the whole world has agreed. (I,10)

<u>Divine or Supernatural Law</u>. Seeing then that all flesh is guilty of that for which God has threatened to punish eternally, what possibility is there of being saved in this way [i.e., by obeying the law]? Therefore, there remains either no way to salvation, or if there is any, then it must surely be a way that is supernatural, a way which could never have entered into the heart of a person even to conceive or imagine unless God himself had revealed it extraordinarily. For this reason we term it the mysterious or hidden way of salvation. (I,11)

The light of nature [reason] is never able to discover any way of obtaining the reward of bliss except by performing exactly the duties and works of righteousness. All flesh being therefore excluded from salvation and life by this route, behold how the wisdom of God has revealed a mystical and supernatural way. … This supernatural way God Himself prepared before all worlds--a way of supernatural duty that He has prescribed for us.… Was there ever any mention made except in that law which God himself has revealed from heaven that there can be no salvation without faith, hope, and love? There is not in the whole world a syllable muttered with certain truth concerning any of these three except what has been supernaturally received from the mouth of the eternal God. Therefore, laws concerning these things are supernatural. (I,11)

Although the Scripture of God is stored with an infinite variety of matter of all kinds, yes, even though it abounds with all sorts of laws, yet the principal intent of Scripture is to deliver the laws of supernatural duties. (I,14)

Natural laws always bind; positive laws do not until after they have been expressly and intentionally imposed. … Positive laws are either permanent or changeable, depending on the purpose for which they were they were first made. Whether God or people are the maker of them, they admit alteration only in so far as their purpose allows. Laws that concern supernatural duties are all positive, and either concern people supernaturally as humans or else as parts of that supernatural society which we call the Church. To affect people supernaturally as humans is to impose duties on them that necessarily belong to everyone and yet which could not have been known by anyone as pertaining to him unless God had revealed them Himself. For these laws do not rest upon any natural or reasonable ground from which they may be deduced, but are ordained by God in order to supply the defect of those natural ways of salvation which we are not yet able to attain. (I,15)

Moral, Ceremonial, and Judicial Laws. We plainly perceive by the difference of those three laws which the Jews received at the hands of God [the moral, the ceremonial, and the judicial] that if the purposes for which God makes His laws always continue one and the same, His laws do also. For this reason, the moral law cannot be altered. Second, whether or not the matters concerning which laws are made continue, if their end has ceased, they also cease to be of force. This is the way it is with the ceremonial law. Finally, even though the end continues, as it does in that specific law against theft as well as in a great part of those other ancient judicial laws, since there is not in all respects the same subject or matter remaining for which they were first instituted, this is sufficient cause for change. And therefore laws, even if ordained of God Himself and even if the purpose for which they were ordained continues, may nevertheless cease if, by alteration of persons or times, they are found inadequate to attain that end. (III,10)

—— *Laying On Of Hands* ——

With prayers of personal benediction, the custom in all ages has been to use the imposition of hands to symbolize our considered desires on behalf of the person we are presenting to God. (V,66)

The Church received from Christ a promise that certain signs and tokens would identify those who believed in Him, including the power to cast out devils, speak in tongues, drive away serpents, be free from the harm of poison, and cure diseases by the laying on of hands. At first this power to heal by imposition of hands was, in some fashion, available to all believers; but they did not all have the same ability to pass on this power to others. Only by the laying on of the Apostles' hands did some of them become instruments for instructing, converting, and baptizing through the gift of the miraculous operations of the Holy Spirit. (V,66)

—— *Liturgy* ——

Consider the irksome deformities of those ministers who are subject to no set order of worship but pray whatever and however they please and frequently disagree in a most insufferable manner with the worthiest parts of Christian worship by their endless and senseless effusions of undigested prayers. (V,25)

Because the Gospels, which we read each week, all declare something that our Lord Jesus Christ either spoke, did, or suffered in His own Person, it has been the custom of Christians to stand out of reverence during its reading, to utter certain words of acclamation, and, at the name of Jesus, to bow. Since no one is required to use these human gestures, we know no reason why anyone should imagine the practice to be an insufferable evil. These ceremonies are useful for showing a reverend regard for the Son of God as being higher than any other messengers who claim to speak for God, and also higher than the infidels, Jews, and Arians who denigrate His honor. (V,30)

The length of our services, which our critics complain so much about, comes to this: if our whole service is read and an hour is allowed for a sermon, we normally spend a half hour more than they do. This extra half hour is apparently of such importance that the age of some and the infirmity of others will not enable them to bear it. If we have any sense of the common ignorance of people, if we care to preserve their wits from being broken by having to pay attention for so long, if we have any love or desire to provide things holy in a manner that will not put people's souls as risk by causing them to loath and abhor what is holy, then this half hour must be eliminated! (V,32)

Our kneeling at Communion is a gesture of devotion. If we presented ourselves to make some stupid show or resemblance of a spiritual meal, then it might be that sitting would be more suitable. Since we come as receivers of an inestimable grace at the hands of God, what could better become our bodies at such an hour than to be physical witness of our minds by being genuinely humbled? Our Lord Himself did that which custom and long usage had made the usual practice at the time. We do that which convenience and decency have made usual practice for us. (V,68)

— *Love* —

That which links Christ to us is His mercy and love for us. That which ties us to Him is our faith in the promised salvation revealed to us in the Word of truth. That which unites and joins us to one another, as though we were of one heart and soul, is our love. (First Sermon on Jude)

If we enter into the search for what God intends to reveal to us we find a thousand testimonies to show that the whole scope of Christ in the work of our deliverance was to display the treasures of His own infinite love, goodness, grace, and mercy. "My sheep I know. I give them eternal life. They shall never perish neither shall anyone pluck them out of My hands." This act of God was sufficient to express the benefit of our deliverance but not sufficient to express God's love for us, and so He added, "Behold, I lay down my life for them." (Sermon on Proverbs/Matthew/ Hebrews)

Even if we ourselves have some immunity from harm, does not true Christian charity require that, if any of our fellows anywhere suffers or is fearful, we count him as our brother? (V,41)

—— *Lutherans (Luther)* ——

The question is not whether an error is made but whether that mistake excludes the possibility of salvation unless it is expressly recanted or repented of. For my part, I dare not deny the possibility of salvation for Lutherans when they have been the chief instrument of our own redemption, even if they do carry to their graves a doctrine [Nestorian heresy] that is greatly repugnant to the truth. (Discourse on Justification)

We can understand how our fathers in the Church of Rome might hold that we are justified by faith alone and at the same time hold, correctly, that without good works, we are not justified.…In this same sense, the Lutherans, in their *Wittenberg Confession* say, "we teach that good works commanded by God are necessary, and that by the free mercy of God they earn their own rewards, either corporal or spiritual." When others [like the Lutherans] speak as our Roman forefathers did, we take their meaning to be sound. (Discourse on Justification)

—— *Marriage* ——

Although single life is more angelical and divine, both the replenishing of the earth with blessed inhabitants and heaven with everlasting saints praising God depends on the intercourse of men and women. (V,73)

He who made all things completely and perfectly saw that it was not good to leave man without a helper and so, in furtherance of His purposes, he chose proportion over perfection and created woman to be man's helper in having and raising children. (V,73)

Human offspring, being of more value than any other in nature, must be nourished with far more care and over a longer period of time to reach maturity than the offspring of any other creature. A man and a woman who are joined for this purpose must, therefore, be tied by a strong and unbreakable knot. This bond of wedlock has always been more or less regarded as something religious and sacred. (V,73)

Since things that are equal in all respects can never be directed by one another, it was impossible that man and woman would agree on anything unless one was superior to the other. Therefore, woman was from the very beginning created by nature later in time and inferior in excellence to man. However, she was formed in so perfect and sweet proportions that as she appears before our eyes she is easier to perceive than define and herein lies the reason why the kind of love that is the most perfect foundation of marriage is rarely susceptible to reason. (V,73)

As for the custom of "giving away" the woman by her father or someone else who had ruled her, we note that in ancient times all women who had no fathers or husbands to govern them had tutors, without whose permission nothing they did was justified. For this reason, they were always delivered to their husbands by other men. This practice reminds women of the duty, required by the constitutional weakness of their sex, to be always directed, guided and ordered by men. (V,73)

The wedding ring has always been used as special pledge of faith and faithfulness. Nothing could be more fitting as a token of our intention to keep a promise that we ought never to break. (V,73)

Of all the marriage rites the one that receives the harshest criticism is the uttering of the words, "With my body I thee worship." Once these words are understood, there will be as little reason to be offended by them as by any of the other marriage customs. In the first place, since unlawful sexual intercourse pollutes and dishonors both parties, this affirmation that we worship and honor one another with our bodies suggests a denial of all impediments and obstacles to knowing one another in the marriage bond without causing any stain or blemish on the marriage. Since this is the likely meaning of the statement, anyone with a quiet and uncontentious mind would approve its use. It is not an absurd conclusion to say that worshipping with the body is the imparting of one's interest in his or her own body to the other--an interest that no one ever had before except the person now bestowing it. This appears more clearly when the other clause was added to the marriage ceremony saying, "With all my worldly good I thee endow." So now we have one promise that offers the principle gift (the person, including the body) and the other that offers what was annexed to it (the social status and economic goods). (V,73)

—— *Martyrs* ——

Those rightly called martyrs are not those who suffer for their disorder and for the ungodly breach which they have caused in Christian unity but those who are persecuted for the sake of righteousness. (Preface, 3.15)

The true martyrs are those who suffer, not on account of wickedness or the impious division of Christian unity, but for the sake of justice. (Autograph Notes, p. 490).

— *Middle Way (See Moderation)* —

There are two opinions concerning the sufficiency of Holy Scripture, each extremely opposite to the other, and both repugnant to the truth. The schools of Rome teach Scripture to be so insufficient that, unless traditions are added, it does not contain all the revealed and supernatural truth that is absolutely necessary for human children to know in this life so that they my be saved in the next. Others, justly condemning this opinion, similarly turn to a dangerous extreme when they hold that the Scriptures not only contain all things necessary for salvation but all ordinary things, in such a way that to do anything according to any other law is not only unnecessary, but even unlawful, sinful, and dangerous to salvation. (II,8)

We cannot excuse any Church that, through corrupt translations of Scripture, delivers ideas that are repugnant to that which God speaks instead of delivering the divine speeches themselves; nor can we excuse any Church which, through false additions, proposes as Scripture to the people of God that which is not Scripture. The blame which, in both of these respects, has been laid upon the Church of England is surely altogether without justification. Concerning translations of Holy Scripture, even though we may not disallow the painful travails of those who have strictly tied themselves to the very original letter of Scripture, yet the judgment of the Church, as we see by the practice of all nations,…has always been that the best translations for a public audience are those which follow a middle course between the rigor of literal translators and the liberty of paraphrases, in such a way that the meaning of Scripture is delivered with the most brevity and greatest clarity of language. (V,19)

In this sense, we can understand how our Fathers in the Church of Rome might hold that we are justified by faith alone and at the same time hold, correctly, that without good works, we are not justified. (Discourse on Justification)

In the matters where the Gentiles were free and the Jews were still tied to their own opinion, the Apostle's doctrine to the Jew was, "Do not condemn the Gentiles"; to the Gentile: "Do not despise the Jew" (Acts 16:4). The one they warned to be careful that scrupulosity did not make them rigorous in giving unadvised sentence against their brothers and sisters who were free; the other they warned not to become scandalous by abusing their liberty and freedom to the offence of their weak brothers and sisters who were being scrupulous. There are two conclusions that may evidently be drawn from this. First, whatever conformity to positive laws the Apostles brought in between the churches of Jews and Gentiles, it was only in those things that might end or continue for a longer or shorter time, as occasion might require. Second, they did not impose upon churches of the Gentiles any part of the Jewish ordinances that required necessary and perpetual observation (as we all acknowledge both by doctrine and practice), except with respect to the convenience and fitness for the present state of the Church as it then was. (IV,11)

There are two things that greatly trouble these later times: one, that the Church of Rome cannot, another that Geneva will not err. (Autograph Notes on *A Christian Letter*, Vol 4, p. 55)

— *Minister (Presbyter/priest)* —

There are four things to be considered in a minister of God: his ordination, which gives him the authority to be involved with sacred elements; the charge or place given him for the exercise of his office; the performance of his duty according to the terms of his charge; and, lastly, the maintenance that he receives. (V,79)

This ministerial power is a mark of separation because it severs those who have it from others and makes them a special *order* that is consecrated to the service of the highest things, in which others are not to meddle. (V,77)

Those who have received the power of ministry may not think to put it on and off like a coat, according to the changes in the weather, or to reject it and then take it back as they see fit. This sort of profane and impious contempt--like other forms of iniquity and apostasy in the Church--has yielded strange behavior. Let those who put their hands to this plough know that, once they are consecrated to God, they are made His personal special inheritance forever. Suspensions may end and degradations of office may completely abolish the use or exercise of ministerial power, but it is not within the power of any man voluntarily to separate and pull apart what God has joined by His authority. (V,77)

Even as the location of common prayer is a condition of its outward form that can help to promote devotion, more important still is the person around whom God's people form themselves in prayer--the one who stands and speaks to God on their behalf. The authority of his position, the fervor of his commitment, the seriousness of his whole demeanor must grace and promote the exercise of his worship of God. (V,25)

The minister holds an office that has been sanctified by God's own blessed grace and ratified by the performance of ministers before him in that office. Is not the minister's very ordination a promise to us that the same divine love that has chosen him will use him as a blessing to his people and accept the prayers he offers up to God on their behalf? (V,25)

Virtue and godly living are necessary qualities in a minister of God because he is expected to teach and instruct his people who are, for the most part, more likely to be led astray by the bad example of one whose life betrays his teaching than to be led in good directions by that teaching. This is true because people are apt to loath and abhor the sanctuary when those who lead the worship service are sinful. (V,25)

Even in the smallest and least significant duties performed by virtue of our ministerial authority, we have a power to dignify, grace, and authorize what no other office on earth can challenge. Whether we preach, pray, baptize, communicate, condemn, give absolution, or whatever we do as disposers of God's mysteries, our words, judgments, acts, and deeds are not our own but the Holy Ghost's. (V,77)

Because while people live they are blessed by God and when they die their works follow them, we must once again call to mind how the worldly peace and prosperity, the secular happiness, the temporal and natural good condition of all people and all governments depend chiefly on religion. There is clear testimony here that, for this reason as well as other, the priest is the pillar of that commonwealth within which he serves God. (V,76)

—— *Ministry: General* ——

The sum of our whole labor in the ministry is to honor God and save man. (V,76)

Religion, without the help of a spiritual ministry, is unable to establish itself. Its fruits cannot grow of their own accord. (V,76)

There is an error that beguiles many who entangle both themselves and others by not distinguishing church *services*, *offices*, and *orders*. The first and part of the second of these may be executed by the laity; but no one can have the third but the clergy. Catechists, exorcists, readers, singers, and others may seem like clergy if we consider only the nature of their work. The Fathers of the Church, for this reason, often called them *clerks*. The goal of many of them was to be ordained once they were qualified by age and experience. These men were not different from other laity except while performing their work, which they might stop doing at any time. Since they were not tied to their work by an irrevocable ordination, we find that they were always clearly distinguished from that group to which the three aforementioned orders were the only rightful parties. (V,78)

Because the ministry is an office of dignity and honor, some doubt that anyone should seek it. [But] as for the order of ministry considered in itself, it has such a bad reputation in the opinion of this present world that those who seek it out need encouragement to bear contempt rather than criticism for being too ambitious. (V,77)

Ecclesiastical power and position may be appropriately desired; the desire may be professed; those who profess themselves inclined in this direction may bring their desires to fruition--all of this without any implication of wrong-doing. (V,77)

Because the burden of the ministry is heavy and the charge laid upon the minister is great, it often happens that even the minds of virtuous men are drawn to very different professions--some of them humbly declining the ministry because of its burdens. At the same time, others fervently and keenly desire the position because of its goodness. There is nothing at all about the ministry that might not lead someone either to shun it with reverence or long for it with deep devotion. (V,77)

We may err if we imagine those to be the least ambitious [for ordination or advancement in the Church] who forebear to stir hand or foot on behalf of their own preferment. There are those who make an idol of their own sufficiency and, because they surmise that the office should be happy to have them in it, they walk around everywhere like some grave pageant, observing whether people do not wonder why so small an account is taken of their worthiness. When other men's advancement is mentioned, they either smile or blush at the amazing folly of the world in not seeing that such dignity should be offered them. (V,77)

Of all the problems I have mentioned about the ministry, the greatest is the three-fold blot or blemish of notable ignorance in the clergy, unconscionable absence from their cures, and insatiable hunting after advancement in the Church without regard or conscience for the public good. (V,81)

What good is it if we in the clergy are learned but lack faith? How does it benefit the Church of Christ if we have ability but do not strive to do that good work that our calling requires of us? (V,81)

The residence of ministers within their own parishes is necessary because, when they are away from the place where they ought to labor, they can neither do the good that is expected of them nor reap the comfort that sweetens life for those who give their lives to their flock. (V,81)

Considering that not an army of twelve thousand learned men would be enough to furnish all the places of worship in this realm, and that our two universities are not enough to replace the number of clergy who die in such great numbers, and that not even a fourth of the parishes provide livings yielding enough income to provide sufficient maintenance for an educated pastor, is it not obvious that, unless most people are to be left completely without the public exercise of religion, there is no remedy but to take into the ministry a number of men who are poorly qualified in terms of their learning? (V,81)

The real question is not whether adequate learning is required in the clergy but whether a Church, within which there is not a sufficient supply of men to supply all the congregations, ought to let thousands of souls grow savage, let them live without any corporate worship, let their children die unbaptized, withhold the benefits of the other sacrament from them, let them depart this world like pagans without anything being read to them about salvation--and all because we lack presbyters who are qualified to preach. (V,81)

I have often heard it asked by many how it might be brought to pass that the Church could everywhere have able preachers to instruct the people, what impediments there are to hinder this development, and what are the speediest ways to remove these impediments. In response, I say that we need to consider the multitude of parishes, the scarcity of colleges, the many discouragements that are offered to men's inclination to be ordained, the extreme poverty of the Church, the irrecoverable loss of so many valuable parish livings of great value that have been entirely taken away from the Church and long since appropriated [by the Crown], the daily pain of failed promotions for clergy, the inadequacy of certain laws concerning the Church, the overreaching power of many bishops, the stony hardness of heart of too many church patrons who lack any sensitivity to these issues. (V,31)

— *Ministry: Orders Of* —

The whole body of the Church is divided between laity and clergy. The clergy, who serve as ministers of Christ's Gospel, are presbyters and deacons. I would prefer to call the first order "presbyters" rather than "priests" only because, in matters of so little moment, I would not wish knowingly to offend the ears of those for whom the word "priest" is so odious--even if there is no good reason for this opinion. (V,78)

Since we are adopted and receive the status of children of God by means of the ministry of those whom God has chosen for this purpose, and since our continuance as His children is under the care of these same men, what better title for them could there be than the reverend name of "presbyter" or fatherly guide? (V,78)

To the two orders of ministry, bishops and presbyters, our Lord and Savior and His Apostles soon added a third: deacons. At first, deacons were stewards of the Church to whom was committed the duty of providing for the poor by distributing the gifts of the Church and the responsibility of assuring that financial affairs were dealt with in a religious and faithful manner. Another part of their office was to assist the presbyters at worship services. (V,78)

There are at this time in the Church of England the same ecclesiastical orders, namely bishops, presbyters, and deacons that had their origin with Christ and His blessed Apostles. As for deans, prebendaries, parsons, vicars, curates, archdeacons, chancellors, officials, commissars, and other similar titles not found in Holy Scripture, we have been thought by some to have admitted these into ecclesiastical orders that were not known in the early church. All of these are, in truth, only titles of offices to which some people who are ordained and some who are not are admitted as the Church may need them. (V,78)

— *Moderation (See Also Middle Way)* —

A moderate and dispassionate temperament, something between fullness and emptiness, has always been thought and found--all things considered--to be the safest and happiest course for everyone to follow, even for kings and princes. (V,76) *Agree*

O happy mixture wherein things that are contrary qualify and correct the dangerous excesses of one another! (V,47)

The world and all things in it are restricted in such a way that all effects that flow from them, all powers and conditions through which they work--whatever they may do, whatever they may be--are limited. This limitation within every creature defines its perfection and assures its preservation. (V,55)

Moderation perfects all things because every thing exists for some reason and cannot serve some end to which it is disproportionate or which is repugnant to it through excess or some other defect. Since nothing perishes except through excess or a defect in that well-proportioned balance and moderation that creates its perfection, it follows that the preservation of all things rest in just this internal equilibrium and harmony. (V,55)

How then does the mind go astray? One's mind is perverse and crooked not when it bends itself toward worldly ends but when it swerves too far either to the right hand or to the left by giving itself over to excesses or to outright defection from the fundamental rule whereby all human actions are judged. That rule, which measures and judges us, is the law of God. (Sermon on Pride)

The virtuous center, or mean, seems to be extreme in the eyes of each extreme. The generous person is, in the opinion of the wasteful person, miserable and, in the judgment of the miserable person, lavish. Impiety, for the most part, upbraids religion as superstitious; superstition accuses it of impiety. Anyone who seeks to reform covetousness or superstition by laboring to achieve its opposite will only draw people out of the lime pit and into the coal bin. (V,65)

Just as a loose tooth causes great grief to a person who tries to eat, so is a loose and unstable word in speech, which is intended to instruct others, offensive. (Discourse on Justification)

If it be asked why God, having infinite power and ability, uses that power in the limited way that we see that He does, the reason is the end which He has proposed for His power. In His wisdom, He has limited the effects of His power by His laws so that His power does not work infinitely but in a way that corresponds with that end for which it works--even in a way that is "the most decent and comely" for "all things in measure, number, and weight." (Wisdom of Solomon 8:1; 11:17). (I,2)

For the singular good of the reestablishment of the whole Church of Jesus Christ, it is most profitable to teach people what is most likely to happen if they quietly consider the trial that has lasted for so long under both kinds of reformation: this moderate kind, which the Church of England has taken, and the other more extreme and rigorous kind which certain churches elsewhere have preferred. In the meanwhile, the suspension of judgment and the exercise of charity may be safer and more seemly for Christian persons. (IV,14)

— *Music* —

Music has an admirable facility to express and represent to the mind, more deeply than any other sensible means, the very standing, rising, and falling steps, turns, and varieties of all the passions to which the mind is subject. (V,38)

The power and pleasing effect that music has on the part of us that is most divine has led some people to conclude that the very nature of the soul is harmony or, at least, that harmony resides within the soul. (V,38)

In musical harmony the very image and character of virtue and vice are perceived. The mind delights in these resemblances and is led to love the things they represent. For this reason there is nothing more contagious and pestilent than some kinds of harmony and nothing more powerfully conducive to good than other kinds of music. (V,38)

Music is something that delights all ages and suits all occasions, is as appropriate in grief as in joy, and is as decent when added to actions of greatest importance and solemnity as when used by people who have removed themselves far from the field of action. (V,38)

At the hearing of some music we are inclined to sorrow and depression. At the hearing of other music our minds are more consoled and softened. One sort is likely to steady and settle us, another to move and stir our emotions. There is music that draws us to a marvelous, grave, and sober moderation. There is music that carries us away, as it were, into ecstasies that fill the mind with a heavenly joy and, for a while, separates us from our bodies. (V,38)

Music can do much to edify, if not our understanding (since this is not an instrument for teaching), then our affections. (V,38)

In church music we desire that beauty and purpose be added to what might otherwise be a merely frivolous, ostentatious, wanton, light, and unstable harmony that pleases the ear but does not further in degree or kind the religious impressions we wish to leave in people's minds. Such music blemishes and disgraces rather than adds to the beauty and force of our service. (V,38)

—— *Ordination* ——

Out of the abundance of His mercy, God has ordained certain persons to attend to the proper execution of the duties and offices necessary for the good of the whole world. Those assigned to this task hold their authority from God, whether invested by God Himself or by the Church in His name. (V,77)

In that ministers are Christ's ambassadors and laborers, who can give them their commission but He whose most intimate affairs they manage? (V,77)

O wretched blindness if we fail to admire great power in the minister, and more wretched still if we recognize it correctly but then suppose that any but God could bestow it! (V,77)

The power that Christ has given to ministers over that mystical body that is the society of souls and over that natural body that He Himself is...is not improperly called a special mark of character, one that is acknowledged to be indelible. (V,77)

The only true and proper act of ordination is to invest men with that power that makes them ministers by consecrating their persons to God and His worship through the use of holy and consecrated elements during the term of their lives--whether they actually exercise this power of or not. To give a minister an entitlement or a charge to serve in a particular place has nothing to do with the making of the minister but only with his placement. (V,80)

Our critics see it as something absurd and unreasonable if a man is ordained a minister unless he is assigned to serve some particular parish. Do they not perceive that by this logic they make it unlawful to employ ministers as missionaries to convert the nations? Of the two types of ordination, the one general and within the church at large, and the other particular to a single congregation, the former is closer to the example of the Apostles. (V,80)

I cannot see what duty ought always to precede ordination except scrutiny of the person's worthiness in terms of his integrity, virtue, and knowledge--and virtue more than knowledge because a defect in knowledge can be remedied but the scandal of a vicious and wicked life is a deadly evil. (V,80)

Our opponents make a mistake when they speak on behalf of a congregation's supposed right to elect their own ministers before the bishop may lawfully ordain them. I dispute the whole idea of popular election of clergy. In any event, the right of patronage drowns whatever the people, under any pretence, might claim as their right to challenge the selection of the pastors who feed their souls. (V,80)

Those who give ordinations should, insofar as they respect the honor of Jesus Christ, the welfare of mankind, and the endless welfare of their own souls, be careful lest unnecessarily and through their fault the Church is found to be worse off and more poorly furnished than it might other wise have been. (V,81)

It has been the opinion of wise and good men that nothing was ever devised of more singular benefit to God's Church than that which our honorable predecessors did--to their endless credit--when they erected houses of study within those two most famous universities [Oxford and Cambridge]. After a reasonable time spent in contemplation, students may enter either into that holy vocation for which they have been nourished and brought up, or they may give way and allow others to occupy their rooms. In this way the Church is always furnished with men whose abilities were first observed in public trial in the work of the Church within the universities, where there are men who are qualified to judge them and to recommend them for suitable callings in the Church at large. All of this is frustrated if the Church is now forbidden to ordain anyone unless he is to serve in some particular parish or congregation. No! Rather than this, would it not be better for us to say of presbyters and deacons that the very nature of their calling is antithetical to local control? (V,80)

Just as no defect in the calling of those who teach the truth can take away the benefit to those who hear it, so the lack of lawful calling in those who baptize cannot make their baptisms without effect for those who receive them. (V,62)

—— *Pastoral Counseling* ——

There are many who labor with great difficulty because the imbecility of their minds does not allow them to censure rightly their own doings. Some are fearful that the enormity of their crimes is so great that no repentance can do them any good. Others fear that the imperfection of their repentance makes it ineffectual for the taking away of sin. … It has therefore pleased Almighty God, in His tender commiseration over these human imbecilities, to ordain for our spiritual comfort consecrated persons who, by granting of power and authority from above, may, as it were, out of God's very mouth support timorous and doubtful minds in their own particular struggles, ease them of all their doubts and scruples, and leave them settled in peace and satisfied concerning the mercy of God towards them. To use the benefit of this help for our better satisfaction in such cases is so natural that it can be forbidden to no person; yet it is not the case that all people stand in need of this help. (VI,6)

—— *Patience* ——

When I say patience I name that virtue which alone has the power to prevent our souls from being overly troubled. This is a virtue most familiar to those who have been chased out of this life in extreme pain. (Sermon on Remedy Against Sorrow and Fear)

Be it ever so hard for us, we must learn to suffer patiently, even that which seems impossible to bear, so that in the hour when God calls us to the final trial and turns this place of honey and pleasure wherein we prosper into that gall and bitterness from which our flesh shrinks, nothing will cause us, in our troubled souls, to rage at, complain about, or resent God. Every heart must be able, with divinely inspired courage, to impress upon itself the lesson: "Be not troubled." (Sermon on Remedy Against Sorrow and Fear)

— *Penitence (See Also Repentance)* —

O Lord, what heaps of grievous transgressions have the most perfect and righteous among us committed and then overlooked without mourning or repenting--and all because the Church has completely forgotten to offer her required services of penitential discipline that give a public example to each individual person of the best way to remember and be drawn into that service of penitence which we have all entirely forgotten as though it were no part of a Christian's duty? (V,72)

Apart from our individual offences, which ought not so loosely be overlooked, do we suppose that the body and corporation of the Church is so moral that it never needs to show itself cast down for those faults and transgressions that, although they do not properly belong to any one person, had a special sacrifice appointed for them in the law of Moses? These sins are common to the whole society that contains everyone. (V,72)

Even as our offences seduce us by giving pleasure, so, by vexing us, punishments seek to reform our transgressions. (V, 72)

Penitence is a prayer that is as acceptable to God whether it is offered in a public setting or in private. However, we may well guess what Christian devotions would come to if people were left to their own voluntary meditations in their private closets and not drawn by laws and orders into the open assemblies of the Church, where they may join in prayer with others. We already know from sufficient experience how little effect it has to tell people about the need to wash away their sins with tears of repentance and then leave them alone to do so. (V,72)

— *Polity, Ecclesiastical* —

Insofar as the Church is the mystical Body of Christ and His invisible spouse, it needs no external polity. That very part of the divine law that teaches faith and the works of righteousness is itself sufficient for the Church of God in this respect. But as the Church is also a visible society and body politic, it cannot lack laws of polity. (III,11)

The matters with which church polity is concerned are the public religious duties of the Church, such as the administration of the Word and sacraments, prayers, spiritual censures, and the like. To these the Church stands always bound. Laws of polity are laws that appoint in what manner these duties shall be preformed. For in the performance of these duties, all who are in the Church cannot work jointly and equally. The first thing required in polity is to differentiate the roles of persons within the Church without which distinctions various functions cannot be executed in an orderly way. Hence, we hold that as long as there is a Church upon earth, God's clergy are, by the plain Word of God Himself, an estate that has been and always will be necessary. (III,11)

—— *Prayer* ——

Prayer is difficult work. (Sermon on Matthew 7.7)

The very wings of prayer are delighted to present our suits in heaven even sooner than our tongues can utter them. (V,33)

Prayers are those children of our lips, those most gracious and sweet aromas, those rich presents and gifts which, being carried up to heaven, give the best testimony of our dutiful affection, (V,23)

Religiously disposed minds are inclined to examine everything of consequence that they do or see according to rules of piety in order to determine what dependency anything has on God, what reference it has to themselves, and what coherence it has with any of the obligations that all earthly things ought to accept. Accordingly, they frame the inward dispositions of their minds sometimes to adore God, sometimes to bless Him and give Him thanks, sometimes to exult in His love, sometimes to implore His mercy. All of these differing elevations of the spirit toward God are contained in the word "prayer." (V,48)

Every good and holy desire, though it lacks correct form, has within itself the substance and force of prayer to God who hears the very moanings, groanings and sighs of our hearts. (V,48)

We make light of the providence of God (though this may be unintentional) and show a lack of mature judgment when we pray in a lazy manner without exerting any effort. (Sermon on Matthew 7.7)

God knows better than we do the best times and the best means and the best things to give us for the good of our souls. (Sermon on Matthew 7.7)

Whoever comes to God with the gift of prayer must do so with a cheerful heart, with a free and frank affection. (Sermon on Matthew 7.7)

Devotion and earnestness add to prayer in the same way that timeliness adds to gifts; they put vigor and life into them. (Sermon on Matthew 7.7)

Prayer proceeds from need which, being heart-felt, makes the suppliant eager. This eager insistence was not only tolerated by our Savior…but also encouraged. Our fervency shows us to be sincerely desirous of what we crave but that which makes us capable of it is a humble spirit. For God bestows his grace upon the lowly; but the proud He sends away empty. (Sermon on Matthew 7.7)

To trust in works without prayer signifies impiety and blasphemy. (Sermon on Matthew 7.7)

When you resolve to seek God do not go out of your house into the street but avoid places of distraction. Separate yourself from yourself, if such is possible. (Sermon on Matthew 7.7)

When you seek God let the love of obedience, the sense and feeling of necessity, and the eye of sincere meaning guide your footsteps and you will not slide. (Sermon on Matthew 7.7)

Let us never stop seeking God. We may be sure that His bounty will be endless, above and beyond our desires. Saul sought an ass and found a kingdom. Solomon named wisdom and God gave him wealth also. God is a giver! (Sermon on Matthew 7.7)

As teaching leads us to know that God is our supreme truth, so prayer testifies that we acknowledge Him to be our sovereign good. (V,23)

Is not the word "prayer" used to signify all of the service we ever do for God? This is so because in religion there is, I suppose, no acceptable duty that does not either presuppose or infer a devout invocation of the name of God. (V,23)

What can we more easily and yet fruitfully bestow upon others than our prayers? If we give advice, only the simple need it; if we give alms, only the poor are relieved; but by prayer, we do good to everyone. (V,23)

When we are unable to do anything else to help our fellows because, through maliciousness or unkindness, they will accept nothing good from our hands, we always have it in our power to bestow prayer and they never have the power to refuse it. (V,23)

Prayer is our means to obtain the graces that God bestows. Our prayers are valid for others as well as for ourselves. To pray for others is to bless them because prayer procures the blessing of God upon them, especially the prayers of those whom God respects, either for their piety and fervor or because their position obligates them to make prayers, as in the case of natural and spiritual fathers. (V,66)

We note that the most pleasant "visitations" sent to us by God have chosen the time of prayer as the most natural opportunity to arrive. (V,23)

According to St Augustine, the brethren in Egypt are reported to have had many prayers, all of them very short, as if they were darts thrown out with a kind of sudden quickness lest that vigilant and erect attention of mind, which in prayer is very necessary, be lost or dulled by long repletion of prayers that were too long and too few in number. (V,33)

Prayer kindles our desire to behold God with our reason. The mind, delighted with that contemplative vision of God, is inflamed to pray. The riches of the mysteries of heavenly wisdom continually stir up in us a desire to move toward God. (V,34)

Though men should speak with the tongues of angels, it is not possible for them to create words so pleasing to the ears of God as those that the Son of God himself has composed. He who taught us to love also taught us to pray, to the end that when we speak to the Father in the Son's words, without any interpretation or gloss of our own, we may be sure that we are uttering nothing that God will either disallow or deny. (V,35)

Because no one's prayer is acceptable whose person is odious and no one who lacks faith is filled with God's grace, it is necessary that all who pray be believers. (V,48)

The petitions of the faithful are often not answered because it is for their own good that they be denied and sometimes the prayers of the faithful are answered even when they seem not to be. (V,48)

To think that we may pray to God for only what He has promised in Scripture is probably an error. We should not ask for things that are in themselves unholy or unseemly. We may, however, wish for whatever nature or grace may move us to seek on behalf of the well being of all people even if God has nowhere promised to grant that for which we pray. (V,48)

When things that are by their nature contingent and changeable are by God's secret will made to happen in a certain way, even if we pray for a different result we are not praying wrongfully because we could not know in advance of God's determination of the event. (V,48)

That Christ, as the only begotten Son of God who had no superior, owed honor to no one, and stood in need of nothing, should make petition to God, might seem most absurd. Yet, in so far as He was a man, expressing either His affection for God or His own needs, what could better become Him than to pray to God? Some things He knew would happen but He prayed for them anyway because He knew that His prayers were the necessary means for bringing them to pass. (V,48)

Preaching (Sermons)

We would greatly wrong a most worthy part of the worship service if we did not highly esteem preaching as the blessed ordinance of God…but we wish to uphold a balanced picture… . (V,22)

Preaching is not the same as teaching in that the objective is not only to teach the truth but also to proclaim the faith. (V,18)

I fail to see how Scripture could possibly be made more accessible to everyone than by a daily reading of extensive parts of it to the people. Much more will be learned this way than through sermons. By reading the whole Book of God every year in church, one can gain much more than by having a small portion of it interpreted each Sunday in sermons. (V,22)

Those churches in which sermons are preached daily, flowing like the sea, display less reverence than is proper to the Living God by this bellowing in the ears of people and by similar substitutes for reading Scripture. (V,22)

Because that which gives sermons their very being is the mind of man, they often taste too much like the corrupt fountain from which they come. (V,22)

As for sermons, be they ever so sound and perfect, they are not God's Word in the sense that the sermons of the Prophets were. No. They are misleadingly called God's Word because God's Word is the subject of and framework for what is usually addressed in sermons. (V,22)

Whenever we conceive a thing in our hearts and thoroughly understand it within ourselves, how great, how long, how earnest is the simplification of it that we are forced to employ before we can utter it in such a way that our brothers and sisters might receive some instruction and comfort from our mouths. After much travail and much pain, when we finally open our lips to speak of the wonderful works of God, our tongues falter within our mouths. Many times we disgrace the dreadful mysteries of our faith and grieve the spirit of our listeners with unsavory words and unseemly speeches. (First Sermon on Jude)

We have good reason to be resentful and fearful lest, by overvaluing sermons, our critics devalue the very worth of Scripture. (V,22)

It seems that Scripture must be *preached*, that is to say, explained by voice and applied to people's lives as the speaker, in his wisdom, thinks best. This alone is what our opponents like to call *preaching*. The bare reading of anything, even Scripture itself, is disliked by our critics, who regard this practice as an ineffectual means to those good ends that we think will result from such readings. (V,21)

Sermons are not the only form of preaching that can save souls. (V,21)

One who does no more than read a lesson from Scripture as part of a service of worship is, by virtue of doing so, preaching. The Apostles in their writing and others in reading in church the Books that the Apostles wrote are not improperly said to be preaching. (V,21)

Preaching is a general instrument that is served both by speaking and reading aloud in Church. True, we do not speak by writing or write by speaking. But what is recorded with the one instrument and uttered with the other may be preached with both. (V,21)

Are we to suppose that St John or the other Gospel writers, in speaking of their intention to instruct and save by their writings, had some secret notion that they never told anyone to the effect that no one in the world could be helped by any sentence they had written until such time as it happened to be preached on or at least set forth in a sermon? (V,22)

Do our critics really want us to believe that faith does not come except by listening to sermons? Surely conversation within the bosom of the Church, religious education, reading the works of learned men, receiving information from church conferences, special diligence and effort in listening to Scripture when it is read in Church, studying the law of God day and night--all of this must have some effect in producing faith in a person. (V,22)

Our critics in their reformed services only indicate the form of service to be used on those days appointed for the *preaching* of the Word, prescribe the words to be said only when the hour appointed for the *sermon* is at hand, and set out what shall be said before and after the *sermon*. According to their format, the standing rule is *no sermon, no service*. This general oversimplification of theirs prompted the French spitefully to term their sort of religion a *mere preach*. (V,28)

Some people encompass all of religion in the single act of hearing a sermon. If they embrace some particular opinion that is different from that held by other people, sermons that fail to uphold that opinion do not please them. (V,81)

Many think that they are obeying the Apostolic canon when, in interpreting sentences of Holy Scripture, they discover everything that is spoken lovingly and positively and then separate these parts from all that is accusatory, sharp and severe. By laboring in this selective and biased manner to "divide the Word," as they put it, our Puritan opponents make the Word a means for dividing and distracting the congregation. (V,81)

The methods used by the Church of England to assure that those who teach others do so soundly, that the purity and unity of historic Christian discipline and doctrine are maintained, and that, avoiding excessive individualism, we all glorify God with one heart and one tongue, are not much approved by those who urge what they call the Apostle's rule and canon upon us. They urge this not so much to assure sound doctrine as to try to prove that non-preaching ministers, as they call them, can have no true and lawful calling in the Church of God. (V,81)

What a minister may lack in knowledge is supplied by those virtues that make his very life an oration that is more worthy than the more learned but less holy speeches of others. (V,81)

So, the question comes down to this: St Paul requires learning in ministers, yes, even such learning as will enable them to teach sound doctrine. May the Church, lacking the qualified ministers that St Paul would have preferred, nevertheless, with good conscience, select from among those with a much lower level of educational background those who have the ability to lead services of corporate prayer, administer the Sacraments to the people, solemnize marriages, visit the sick, bury the dead, and instruct the people by reading Scripture and prepared homilies--even though they are not as yet qualified to benefit and feed Christ's flock by their preaching? (V,81)

— *Predestination* —

All things that God brought forth in the times and seasons of His chosen people existed eternally before all time within God, just as a work not yet begun is within the mind of a workman before he creates it at some later time. Whatever we behold now in this present world was folded in the bowels of divine mercy, written in the book of eternal wisdom, and held in the hands of the omnipotent power before the first foundations of the world were laid. They are *in Him* as effects of their original cause. He is likewise *in them*; the support and influence of His deity is their very life. (V,56)

There are those who elevate too highly a simple and immediate means of new life relying solely on the single idea of predestination and subordinating those means without which we are not actually brought to enjoy what

God secretly intended. It is but self-deceiving vanity to trust in God's election of us if we do not keep ourselves in the paths that God appointed for us to walk in. (V,60)

It is by means of the sacraments and other visible tokens of grace that we are able to know that He, whose mercy granted us in this life the means to eternal life, long ago intended us to that end to which these tokens lead. Let us never think it safe to presume our predestination to life eternal by mere conjectures about God's intention and purpose without attention to the means to that end. (V,60)

Other, non-thinking, things also have purposes for which they exist. But they lack the faculty to know, judge, or treasure these purposes and thus they achieve them unwittingly. Similarly, the means they use to achieve their appointed ends are predetermined and so they cannot turn away from them. For example, the purpose for which the heavens move they know not; nor can they help but continue their motions. Only humans, in all their actions, know what it is they seek and are not bound by any predetermined means to achieve those ends. In the whole world, no creature but man has the ultimate purpose of his actions held out for him as a recompense and reward. If his mind chooses that purpose, he is thought to have a right or straight mind; if not, his mind is called perverse. (Sermon on Pride)

Predestination does not bring us to life eternal without the grace of an actual calling of us--which implies Baptism. Even as we are not men by nature without human birth, so neither are we Christians in the eyes of God's Church without a new birth. (V,60)

It follows, therefore, (1) that God has predestined certain human beings, not all; (2) that the cause that moved God to do so was not the foresight of any virtue in us at all; (3) that to Him the number of His elect is definitely known; (4) that it must be that those to whom the purpose of God's saving grace does not extend are condemned by their sins; (5) that to God's foreknown elect absolute assurance of salvation final is given; (6) that the inward grace which is necessary for anyone to be saved is not given to all people; (7) that no person comes to Christ who is not drawn by God through the inward grace of his Spirit; and (8) that it is not in any person's mere ability, freedom and power to be saved, for no person's salvation is possible without grace. (Dublin Fragments)

—— *Pride (Sin)* ——

Nature works in us all a love of our own counsels. The contradiction of others is a fan to inflame that love. Our love is set on fire to maintain that which we have done, to sharpen the wit to dispute, to argue, and by all means to reason for it. (Pref. 2,7)

Pride is a vice that attaches itself so firmly to the hearts of men that if we were to strip ourselves of all faults but one we would, without doubt, find pride the last and hardest one to cast off. (Sermon on Pride)

Although people are not proud of anything that is not valued by public opinion, neither are they proud of anything thus valued unless it is possessed by only a few and desired by all. Only such scarce goods, we believe, will bring honor to those who have them. (Sermon on Pride)

Pride is nothing but an inordinate elation of the mind that proceeds from a false conception of a person's excellence in honorable things which, in turn, frames his opinion of ALL his deeds and behavior, unless he is cunning enough to conceal it. A foul scar may be covered with a fair cloth. As proud as Lucifer is, he may in outward appearance be humble. (Sermon on Pride)

Whatsoever harm comes to families because of disobedience of children, stubbornness of servants, intractableness of wives (who though in all other things they may rule are still subject because of the inequality of their sex), or whatever harm comes from strife among people within the fellowship of various communities, or from the tyranny of rulers, the ambitions of nobles, the rebellion of subjects, the heresies, schisms, and divisions within the church--in all these situations when we name *pride*, we name the mother that brought them forth and the only nurse that feeds them. (Sermon on Pride)

Give me the hearts of all people humbled and what is there that can overthrow and disturb the peace of the world? Although many things are the cause of much evil, pride is the cause of all evil. (Sermon on Pride)

So hard it is to cure a sickness like pride because the very remedies that cure vices cause this one. If we were clean of all spots and blemishes, including pride itself, we might still be proud that we were not proud. Thus it is often God's wisdom to suffer a just person to fall so that, being raised up again, he may learn what power it is that upheld him. (Sermon on Pride)

I am not afraid to affirm boldly, with St. Augustine, that people who are puffed up with a proud opinion of their own righteousness and holiness may actually benefit when God, in His grace, permits them to sin grievously. By this means their excessive liking of themselves may be supplanted with a more realistic dislike of themselves. (Sermon on Pride)

— *Psalms* —

The Psalms contain and express more briefly and movingly the best and most beautiful that is in other books of Scripture. They do so because of the poetical form in which they are written. (V,37)

What is there that is necessary for us to know that the Psalms are unable to teach? For beginners they are an easy and familiar introduction; for those already of the faith, they provide a mighty increase of the same; and, for the most perfect, they offer a strong confirmation. (V,37)

There is no grief that invades the soul of man, no wound or sickness you can name for which there is not to be readily found in this treasure house an available and comfortable remedy. (V,37)

Heroic magnanimity, exquisite justice, grave moderation, exact wisdom, unfeigned repentance, the mysteries of God, the terrors of God's wrath, the comforts of Grace, the works of Providence over this world, and the promised joys of that world which is to come, everything good that needs to be known, done, or had is yielded in this one celestial fountain. (V,37)

— *Reason* —

I take it there is a difference between a talk that suits nursing children and their nurses and that by which persons of capacity do--or should--receive instruction. (Sermon on Pride)

There are some people who think that they cannot admire as they should the power and authority of the Word of God if they attribute any force to human reason in things divine. In such a case, they never use reason so willingly as to disgrace reason. (III,7)

The will must be, in all things, controlled by reason and reason must be directed by the laws of God and nature. (Sermon on Pride)

Our nature being much more delighted to be led than pulled, we stubbornly resist authority many times over, while to persuasion we yield easily. Thus, the wisest lawmakers have always endeavored to make those laws seem reasonable that they most wanted to have inviolably obeyed. Simple law commanding or forbidding is but dead compared to one that expresses the reasons why it commands or forbids. And surely, even concerning the laws of God, although His commandment is in itself reason enough to exact total obedience at the hands of people, there is a strong inducement to obey with greater alacrity and cheerfulness of mind when we see plainly that nothing is imposed to which we must yield unless we are being unreasonable. In a word, whatever we are taught, be it a precept for direction of our manners, or articles for instruction of our faith, or a document intended to inform our minds, it takes root and abides in us when we conceive not only what God has spoken but why. (Sermon on Pride)

The mind conceives Christ by hearing Christian doctrine, even as the light of nature causes the mind to grasp those truths that are merely rational. So the saving truth, which is far above the reach of human reason, cannot be conceived except through the operation of the Almighty. (Discourse on Justification)

—— *Reformers (Reformation)* ——

So I come to those accusations brought against us by the pretenders of reformation. If the Church today were really as corrupted as the most prominent among these reformers imagine, I would exhort every person in it to seek God's pardon, with tears in his eyes. (V,4)

We trust that God's mercy will be our safeguard against these enraged reformers who have become our principal enemies. (V,4)

—— *Religion* ——

We can find no people anywhere in the world who have lived without religion. (V,18)

True religion is the root of all virtue and the foundation of all well ordered commonwealths. (V,1)

Religion not only gives life and perfection to all endeavors with which it is mingled, but whatever events proceed from it yield, if not joy and gladness, then always patience, satisfaction, and reasonable peace of mind. (V,1)

So natural is the union of religion with justice that we may boldly deny that there is either where both are not. For, how can they be unfeinedly just whom religion does not cause to be so, or how can they be religious who are found not to be so by the justice of their actions? (V,1)

The well being of all people depends upon religion. Religion, when truly embraced, directs people's behavior toward all sorts of virtuous service to the commonwealth. (V,1)

People are much more effectively restrained from doing evil by their fear of God than by any positive laws because those laws only have power over their actions whereas their inner thoughts, private intentions, and inclinations of heart are more effectively bridled by religion. (V,2)

—— *Repentance (See Also Penitence)* ——

Repentance is the chief end of spiritual authority. There are two kinds of repentance: the one a private duty toward God, the other a duty of external public discipline....By repentance, we are to appease those whom we offend by sin. Since all sins deprive us of the favor of Almighty God, our way of reconciliation with Him is the inward secret repentance of the heart. This inward repentance alone suffices, unless some special quality of the sin committed or in the party that has done amiss requires more. For besides our submission in God's sight, repentance must not only address the private harm done to others, if the sin be an injurious crime, but must extend further to the wholesome discipline of the Church which demands a more exemplary and public satisfaction. Since the Church is as satisfied with outward repentance as God is with inward, it is appropriate for the sake of clarity always to call the latter the "virtue" of repentance, and the former the "discipline" of repentance. (VI,3)

The virtue of heart-felt repentance is God's handiwork, a fruit or effect of divine grace…. The whole chain of virtues implied in the name of grace are infused at one instant, yet when they meet and concur in us, they each have their distinct operation which arises in orderly fashion. It is, therefore, necessary that we note the way or method of the Holy Spirit in framing peoples' sinful hearts to repentance…. Hence, the wellspring of repentance is faith, first breeding fear, and then love. This love causes hope, and hope leads to the resolution to attempt reconciling action. (VI,3)

The following are required in a penitent's or convert's duty: first, the aversion of the will from sin; second, the submission of ourselves to God by supplication and prayer; and third, the intention to lead a new life attested by good works. These three things are well compressed into one definition by those who say that repentance is a virtue that hates, bewails, and shows a purpose to amend sin. We offend God in thought, word, and deed. The first offence is corrected by contrition, the second by confession, and the last, by our works of satisfaction. (VI,3)

— Rest (From Labor) —

Rest is the end of all motion and the final perfection of all things that labor. Labor for us is a journey that brings not happiness until it brings rest. (V,70)

Let us not confuse rest with idleness. They are idle who avoid labor because of the pain of doing the work that God and nature bind them to. They are at rest who either end their work when they have brought it to perfection, or else cease a lesser task because a worthier and better one is to be undertaken. God has created nothing to be idle or improperly employed. (V,70)

—— *Resurrection* ——

This life and this resurrection in our Lord Jesus Christ are available to all people because of what Christ has done for us. That which makes us partakers of what is offered is our individual communion with Christ. The sacrament of Communion is a primary means to strengthen that bond with Christ and so to multiply in us the fruits of this communion with Him. (V,68)

Even when His soul left the tabernacle of His body, Christ's deity forsook neither body or soul. If it had, we could not then truly hold either that the person of Christ was buried or that the person of Christ raised itself up from the dead. The body separated from the Word can in no true sense be termed the person of Christ. Nor is it true to say that the Son of God, in raising up that body, was raising up Himself, if that body were not both with Him and of Him during the time when it lay in the tomb. The same may be said of the soul. (V,52)

—— *Revelation: Private* ——

Whenever one is moved to rely on the singularity of God's revelation to him, he ought to suspect his own motives. (V,10)

If the Church gave each person license to follow whatever practice he imagined God's spirit had revealed to him alone, or to some special person whom he esteems highly, what result could possibly ensue but utter confusion in the Church--all under the pretence of one person's claim to be specially taught, led, and guided by God's spirit. (V,10)

When we examine the errors and the general inadequacy of arguments for following private revelations of God's intentions, we see a strong presumption that God has not in fact spoken to the hearts of those who make such claims because he has not given them the ability to prove their assertions. (V,10)

Consider the manifold confusions that befall all those who think that every person's individual spirit or gift (as they call it) is the only bishop that ordains them to their ministry. (V,25)

— *Righteousness* —

There neither is nor ever was any purely natural person who was absolutely righteous, devoid of all unrighteousness, of all sin. We dare not exempt from this truth the Blessed Virgin herself. Even she, the mother of the Redeemer, is not, apart from Christ's redemption of her, released from the bond of sin. If Christ paid a ransom for all, even for her, it follows that all, without exception, are captives of sin and that no one is righteous in himself. (Discourse on Justification)

We are absolutely righteous in Christ. In Christ we have wisdom, justice, sanctification, and redemption: wisdom because He revealed His Father's will to us;

justice because He offered Himself as a sacrifice for our sins; sanctification because He has given us His spirit; redemption because He has appointed a day to deliver His children out of the bondage of corruption into a glorious liberty. (Discourse on Justification)

The righteousness of sanctification is different from the righteousness of justification. We do not deny that the righteousness of sanctification is inherent and that we must work to achieve it. We are righteous in one way by the faith of Abraham and in the other by the works of Abraham. Of the one way St. Paul says, "To him who does no works but believes, faith yields righteousness." On the other hand, St. John says, "He is righteous who does the works of righteousness." St. Paul shows that by Abraham's example we have righteousness by faith without works. But St. James says that by Abraham's example one is justified by works along with faith. We see that St. Paul clearly severs these two aspects of Christian righteousness from one another in the second chapter of Romans where he writes, "Being freed from sin and made servants of God you have your fruits in holiness and, at the end, everlasting life." (Discourse on Justification)

—— *Roman Catholics* ——

The Church of Rome should be regarded as a part of God's House, a limb of the visible Church of Christ. (V,68)

As for charges of so-called "imitation of papists" and "breeding of superstition," these are now such common guests in our house that no one can think it discourteous to let them leave as they came. (V,71)

To say that we may in no way follow the usage of the Church of Rome is violent and extreme. There are some things they do in that they are human, some in that they are wise and Christian people, some in that they are misled and blinded by error. Insofar as they follow reason and truth we are not afraid to tread in the same steps they have trod and to be their followers. (V,28)

Whereas Rome retains what is ancient and better, we see others leaving these practices for new ones and changing things for the worse. We would be better off following the perfection of those whom we do not like than imitating the errors of those we love. (V,28)

We believe it much better to stay with the practice of the Church of Rome and establish a prescribed form of worship that everyone is required to observe rather than to go with those who set down some general outline that ministers may use or not as they choose, or change in any way that pleases them. (V,28)

If anything moves the Roman Catholics to strengthen their faith, we should not quench with delays and jealousies that feeble aura of conformity that breathes out from them, but build on whatever foundation there may be in them, add perfection to slender beginnings and, as with other offices of worship, offer them this Eucharistic food of life that Christ has given His Church, not only for preservation of strength but also for relief of weakness. (V,68)

Since the Church of Rome is as corrupted in faith as it is, refusing to be reformed, as it does, we must sever ourselves from it. Even the example of our fathers in the Roman Church may not keep us in communion and fellowship with that Church in the hope that by so doing we and they might be saved. (Discourse on Justification)

I do not doubt that God was merciful to save thousands of them [Roman Catholics], although they lived in popish superstition, because they sinned out of ignorance. (Discourse on Justification)

Do we know how many millions of our fathers in the Roman Church may have ended their mortal lives by uttering, before their breath ceased, "Christ, my Savior, my Redeemer, Jesus"? Shall we say of them that they did not hold to the foundation of Christian faith? (Discourse on Justification)

Shall we lap them all [Roman Catholics] up in one condition? Shall we cast them all without distinction headlong into the pit? Shall we plunge them all into that infernal and ever-flaming lake--those who have been merely participants in maintaining error along with those who have committed heretical acts, those who were the authors of heresy along with those who, by terror or violence, were forced to receive it, those who have taught heresy along with those simple folk who were seduced into believing error by the rhetorical tricks of false teachers, those who partook of one heresy along with those who partook of many, those of many with those of all? ...Woe is the hour wherein we were born unless we can persuade ourselves of better endings --even of salvation for them, although we know that condemnation is due. We must show some way that our unwitting if sinful forefathers [in the Roman Church] might escape eternal damnation. There is but one way, and that is by appealing to the seat of God's saving mercy. (Discourse on Justification)

We can understand how our fathers in the Church of Rome might hold that we are justified by faith alone and at the same time hold, correctly, that without good works, we are not justified. … In this same sense, the Lutherans, in their *Wittenberg Confession*, say, "we teach that good works commanded of God are necessary and that by the free mercy of God they earn their own rewards, either corporal or spiritual." When others [like the Lutherans] speak as our Roman forefathers did, we take their meaning to be sound. (Discourse on Justification)

Charity requires that, since our Roman forefathers' meaning is uncertain, we should give a favorable rather than an unfavorable construction to their words. Even if we accept the worst construction, namely that all of them embraced the false doctrine [justification by works] while alive, might not we suppose that many of them renounced the heresy at the time of their death? After all, when people feel easy about themselves, they vainly tickle their fancies with who knows what reckless ideas about the connection between their merits and their rewards, which, in the trance of high speculations, they dream God has weighed up and laid out, as it were, in bundles for them. Nevertheless, we see by daily experience that some people, as the hour of death approaches, as they hear themselves summoned to appear and stand at the bar of the Judge whose brightness causes the eyes of the angels themselves to be dazzled, begin to hide the faces of their idle imaginations. To name their merits at such a time is to lay their souls open to the rack. The memory of their deeds is then loathsome to them. They forsake everything in which they had previously put their trust and confidence. There is no staff to lean upon, no ease, no rest, no comfort then, except in Christ Jesus. (Discourse on Justification)

The most learned opinions hold that all the heresies and corruptions of the Church of Rome do not prove that it directly denied the foundation of the faith. If that had been proved, then that church would simply be no Christian Church at all. Even Calvin said that in the papal church something of the true Church remains, a church crazed, if you will, broken quite into pieces, forlorn, misshapen, yet still a church. Calvin's reasoning was that before faith is utterly denied, the Antichrist must 'sit in God's Temple.' (Discourse on Justification)

Give me a person of whatever estate or condition, yes even a cardinal or a pope, ...am I to think that because of this single error [that man is justified by his good works] such a person cannot so much as touch the hem of Christ's garment? Should I not, in such a case, hope that Christ's virtue might save him? Simply because his error indirectly overthrows the foundation of faith, shall I cast him out as one who has cast off Christ, as one who holds to Christ by not even a lender thread? No. I will not be afraid to say even to a cardinal or a pope in this situation, 'Be of good comfort. Ours is a merciful God.' Ours is a God who makes the most of what little faith we have, not a capricious sophister who gathers up the worst of our mistakes. (Discourse on Justification)

Let me die if ever it be proved that simple error in such a case [holding the doctrine of justification by works] excludes a pope or a cardinal from all hope of eternal life. Surely I must confess to you that if it be an error to think that God may be merciful to save us when we err, then my greatest comfort is my error. Were it not for the love I bear to this error, I would neither wish to speak nor to live. (Discourse on Justification)

— *Sabbath* —

If the Jews did so reverence their Sabbath, which was but a shadow of ours, are not we who inhabit the light and truth of Grace bound to honor that day which the Lord himself honored and on which He delivered us from both dishonor and death? Are we not bound to keep it singular and inviolable? Is it not a reckless neglect of religion to make that very day ordinary and to think that we may do with it as we do with all the rest? (V,71)

On those rare occasions when our individual affairs are subject to obvious harm unless we continue to peruse them, we may, with a very clear conscience, ignore the usual rules about keeping the Sabbath, in light of our Savior's dispensation which He grounded on the axiom, "Man was made for the Sabbath; the Sabbath was not made for man." (V,71)

— *Sacraments* —

Sacraments serve as God's instruments of grace. (V,57)

Sacraments are powerful instruments of God for eternal life. (V,50)

It has been said that there are three things that make up the substance of a sacrament: the grace that is offered, the elements that signify that grace, and the words that express what is done by the elements. (V,58)

The grace that comes through or with the sacraments comes not from the sacraments but from God. (V,57)

The sacraments contain in themselves no vital force or efficacy. They are not physical instruments. They are moral instruments for salvation and duties of service and worship. (V,57)

Generally, a truly religious sacrament is every admirable thing which divine authority has taught God's Church either to believe or observe. It comprehends something not otherwise understood except by faith alone. (Dublin Fragments, Vol. IV, p.115)

In a word, sacraments are God's secrets revealed to none but his own people.... It is therefore required that a sacrament, in this sense, be (1) a perpetual duty in religion and, for a Christian sacrament, that it be proper to Christian religion; (2) that Christ be the author thereof; (3) that all people be bound to receive it; (4) that it have a promise from God for the receiver; (5) that there be in it a visible sign, expressing the grace being accomplished through the death of our Savior Christ, who is to us the fountain of all grace; and (6) that all these things concerning it be apparent in Holy Scripture, because they are all supernatural truths which cannot otherwise be demonstrated. (Dublin Fragments, Vol. IV, p. 115)

There is, in addition to the matter and form in which the essence of a sacrament consists, a certain outward form whereby the same is decently administered. The substance of all religious action is delivered from God Himself in few words. For example, St. Augustine says this about a sacrament: "Unto the element let the word be added, and they both make a sacrament." Baptism is given by the element of water along with that prescribed form of words which the Church of Christ uses. The sacrament of the body and blood of Christ is administered in the elements of bread and wine, along with those mystical words that are added to it. (IV,1)

We do not take Baptism or the Eucharist to be mere resemblances or memorials--hidden or naked signs and testimonies given to assure us of grace received in the past. Rather, when we receive the sacraments we take them to be--as indeed they in truth are--effective means whereby God gives us that grace which assures us of eternal life. (V,57)

Sacraments serve as bonds of obedience to God, strict obligations to the mutual exercise of Christian charity, provocations to godliness, preservations from sin, and memorials of the principal benefits we receive from Christ. The sacraments also provide security from weakness of faith and are marks of distinction that separate God's people form others. (V,57)

Sacraments are heavenly ceremonies that God has sanctified and ordained to be administered in His Church, first as signs to show us when and where He imparts the vital and saving grace of Christ to all who are capable of receiving Him and, secondly, as a service that God requires of those to whom He imparts His grace. Since God's Person is invisible and cannot be discerned by us, it seemed good, in the eyes of His heavenly wisdom, that we should be able, for some particular purpose, to recognize His glorious presence. He gave us this simple and reasonable token whereby we might know what we cannot see. (V,57)

Not everyone who receives the sacraments will receive God's grace, even though it is not usually His will to bestow the grace of the sacraments on anyone except by means of the sacraments. (V,57)

There are two elements to be observed in sacraments: their inner power and their outer force. The necessity for us rests in their power. We cannot discover in what sense they are necessary until we see just how they are effective in our lives. When sacraments are said to be visible signs of invisible grace, we understand that grace is indeed the purpose for which these heavenly mysteries were instituted. (V,50)

We are greatly offended when people labor to show us the usefulness of the Holy sacraments and assign to them no purpose other than to instruct our minds by use of other senses than those which the Holy Word uses to teach us through the sense of hearing. If the only benefit we reap from the sacraments is instruction, we will surely hold them in less estimation than Scripture. There is in the sacraments undoubtedly a more excellent and heavenly purpose than instruction. (V,57)

Sacraments, by reason of their mixed nature, are more diversely interpreted and disputed than any aspect of worship. Since such a great store of reality is contained in a sacrament, each person's imagination takes hold of some part as being most important. This results in much disagreement among the many opinion about why sacraments are necessary. (V,57)

We can never know, nor are we required to examine, what is in every person's private mind about the sacraments. It is sufficient that we follow the general teaching of the Church and assume that anyone who outwardly conforms to the Church's direction in this matter has inwardly satisfied the purposes of God's Church. (V,58)

As for the sacraments themselves, from all we can gather from that which is written about them in Scripture, they exhibit but do not actually contain within themselves that grace that it pleased God to bestow with them or through them. (V,67)

We admire the goodness of God in nature when we consider how He assured that what was most necessary to preserve life would be quick and easy for all living creatures to come by. Is it not an evident sign of His wonderful providence when that food of eternal life, without which our endless death and destruction would ensue, is prepared and always set before us in such a readily available form that nothing could be easier than the means he provides for us to procure it? (V,22)

— *Salvation* —

This longing to be saved, without understanding the true way to do it, has been the cause of all the superstitions in the world. (Discourse on Justification)

It is our wisdom and our comfort. We care for no knowledge in the world but this: that man sinned and God suffered, that God made Himself the sin of man, and that men are made the righteousness of God. (Discourse on Justification)

[We are asked]…to believe the improbable truth that our salvation comes through a man who seemed outwardly to be forsaken by God, judged and condemned by the wicked, buffeted on the face, scoffed at by soldiers, scourged by tormentors, hanged on a cross, pierced in the heart, heard by many witnesses to roar, in the anguish of His soul--as if His heart had been rent asunder--"Oh, my God, why have You forsaken me?" I say to you that such a doctrine of salvation seems so improbable to a reasonable person that if we preach it to the Gentile or to the Jew, the one will condemn our faith as madness, the other as blasphemous (First Sermon on Jude).

Our minds are subject to that which we most abhor: anguish, tribulation, death, woe, endless misery. For whatever misses the mark of true life will end in perdition. Since everyone is wrapped up in sin and made thereby a child of death, the minds of all being plainly judged not right, shall we then think that God endued His creatures with so many excellent qualities only to leave them in such a state that they never be happier than if they had never existed? Now there comes a new way of salvation, so that those who were in the perverse mode may be found to be straight and righteous. The old perverse way is the way of nature. The new way is the way of grace. (Sermon on Pride)

The fulfillment of the way of nature is salvation earned, presupposing the righteousness of our works, a righteousness grounded in the natural inclination to do good works that God implanted in us. But the way of salvation bestowed upon us by God as a gift does not presuppose our righteousness but the forgiveness of our unrighteousness. (Sermon on Pride)

The very nature of Christian belief, the life and soul of Christ's Gospel, rests in this: that by ignominy honor and glory is obtained; power is vanquished by imbecility; and, by death, salvation is purchased. (Sermon on Hebrews)

If anyone is deprived of deliverance, the fault is his own. Let no one, therefore, probe the clouds looking for hidden impediments to his salvation. Let them not, like the infidels and heathens, stormily impute their wretched condition to destiny. … The fatal bar that closes the door to God's saving mercy is only our willful contempt of the grace and salvation offered to us. (Sermon on Hebrews)

Upon this sure foundation let us, therefore, build: Christ died to save us *all*. … You have the plainly expressed words of our Lord and Savior inviting *all* unto Him who labor. You have the blessed Apostle's assertion that Christ by His death defeated Satan to the end that He might deliver *all* who are held in bondage. Urge this upon yourself: God cannot deny Himself. He preaches deliverance, by His death, for *all*. (Sermon on Hebrews)

If any are not saved it is because they have said to their own hearts, "Our present pleasures will remain our god; we care not for this offered favor; we will not have Him to be our deliverer." If people like this perish, what eye is there to pity them? (Sermon on Hebrews)

Our first embracing of Christ is our first rebirth from the state of death and condemnation. (Discourse on Justification)

Is it my meaning that nothing is required for salvation but Christ's silent action? No. We acknowledge no such doctrine. Rather, I teach what I myself have been taught, namely that, in addition to that bare, naked work wherein Christ without any other associate purchased our salvation, the actual conveyance to us of this great blessing requires much more. It requires that we were known and chosen by God before the foundation of the world, justified in this life, and after our deaths, sanctified and received by God in heaven. None of this means that we are not required to act also. Our vocation is to listen to the Gospel, express the fruits, or works, of the Spirit,

162

and persevere in hope, faith, and holy living. (Discourse on Justification)

— *Schism* —

The conflicts within the Church are often over matters of no small importance leading to schism, factions, and other evils to which the body of the Church is subject. The healthy and the sick alike should remain in the same body so long as each retains, by outward profession, that vital substance of truth that distinguishes the Christian religion from religions that do not acknowledge that our Lord Jesus Christ is the Blessed Savior of mankind, give no credence to the glorious Gospel, and hold in derision his sacraments, which are the guarantors of salvation. (V,68)

Schismatics, through the quarrels over which they divide themselves from their brethren, have forsaken the true Church of God. Yet they have not completely left or forsaken the Church in terms of the main foundation of the faith in which they may continue to believe, even though they have torn asunder the rest. (V,68)

— *Scripture (Bible)* —

Unless there is a clear contradiction between the words in the translation and the intent of the Scriptural passage, we should not regard every little discrepancy as an intolerable blemish that must be expunged. (V,19)

With us there is never a time when we have divine services without reading from Scripture. We count this as the most necessary thing. We would not dare allow any form of liturgy that required no Scripture, or only a little of it, to be read out in church. (V,20)

The purpose of the Word of God is to *save*. Therefore we call it *the Word of life*. The way for people to be saved is through knowledge of that truth which is taught in God's Word. Since eternal life is available to everyone, it follows that the Word of God, which is the necessary means to salvation, must be available to all. In this sense, the Word of Life has always been a treasure that, though precious, is as easy to attain as it is to understand. (V,21)

Since God, who knows and discloses the rich treasures of His wisdom, has chosen Scripture as the most effective means to impart His treasures to the world, it follows that Scripture must be fully and perfectly understandable in and of itself in those areas that impart knowledge of everything essential for the attainment of eternal life. (V,21)

Miraculous and strange effects may result from unlikely means but did we ever hear it regarded as a wonder that a person who reads Scripture comes to believe and live according to the will of almighty God? (V,22)

Scripture is not so difficult that reading alone [in church] is insufficient to give eternal life to willing listeners. (V,22)

There are two opinions concerning the sufficiency of Holy Scripture, each extremely opposite to the other, and both repugnant to the truth. The schools of Rome teach Scripture to be so insufficient that, unless traditions are added, it does not contain all the revealed and supernatural truth that is absolutely necessary for human children to know in this life so that they my be saved in the next. Others, justly condemning this opinion, similarly turn to a dangerous extreme when they hold that the Scriptures not only contain all things necessary for salvation but all ordinary things, in such a way that to do anything according to any other law is not only unnecessary, but even unlawful, sinful, and dangerous to salvation. (II,8)

We cannot excuse any Church which, through corrupt translations of Scripture, delivers ideas that are repugnant to that which God speaks, instead of delivering the divine speeches themselves; nor can we excuse any Church which, through false additions, proposes as Scripture to the people of God that which is not Scripture. The blame which, in both of these respects, has been laid upon the Church of England is surely altogether without justification. Concerning translations of Holy Scripture, even though we may not disallow the painful travails of those who have strictly tied themselves to the very original letter of Scripture, yet the judgment of the Church, as we see by the practice of all nations, …has always been that the best translations for a public audience are those which follow a middle course between the rigor of literal translators and the liberty of paraphrases, in such a way that the meaning of Scripture is delivered with the most brevity and greatest clarity of language. (V,19)

God himself cannot possibly err nor lead human beings into error. For this reason, whatever He affirms in His testimonies is always the truth and a most infallible certainty.   Further, because the things that proceed from Him are perfect without any manner of defect or deformity, it cannot be otherwise than that the words of His mouth are absolute and lack nothing which they should have for performing that thing whereunto they tend. From this it follows that, since the end to which He directs His speech is known, even a negative argument is always strong and forcible concerning those things that are apparently a prerequisite for the same end. (II,1)

Some acts are permitted in such a way that they are actually required as necessary for salvation. They are of such immediate, direct, proper and final necessity that, without performance of them, we cannot by any ordinary course be saved; nor can we by any means be excluded from life by observing them. In actions of this kind our principal direction is from Scripture; for nature is no sufficient teacher of what we should do in order to attain life everlasting. The insufficiency of the light of nature is by the light of Scripture so fully and so perfectly supplied that no further light than this is needed for that end. (II,8)

Being persuaded by other means that these Scriptures are the oracles of God, we hold that they themselves lay before us all the duties that God requires at our hands as necessary for salvation.… Now there has been sufficient reason alleged to conclude that all things necessary for salvation must be made known and, further, that God himself has therefore revealed His will. Otherwise humans could not have known what is necessary for salvation. God's ceasing to speak to the world since the publishing of the Gospel of Jesus Christ, and the delivery of the same in writing, is to us a clear evidence that the way of salvation is now sufficiently revealed and that we need no other means for our full instruction than God has already furnished us with. (I,14)

Scripture teaches us the saving truth that God has made known to the world by revelation, and it presumes that we are taught in other ways that are also divine and sacred. The question then is by what means we are taught this. Some answer that we have no other way to learn it than by tradition, so that we believe because we have learned from our predecessors who have learned it from theirs. But is this enough? That which experience teaches all humans may not be denied. By experience we all know that the first outward motive leading persons so to esteem Scripture is the authority of God's Church. For when we know the whole Church of God has that opinion of Scripture, we judge it to be an impudent thing for any person bred and brought up in the Church to be of a contrary mind without cause. (III,8)

I hold it as an infallible rule in interpreting Scripture that, where a literal construction will stand, the further we move away from the word itself, the worse will be our understanding. There is nothing more dangerous than this licentious and self-deluding artifice that changes the meaning of words, the way alchemy would change the substance of metals, and makes out of something anything it pleases, thereby bringing all truth to nothing. While we might bear with such free exercise of imagination in other matters, in important matters like this one, which deal with regeneration by water and the Holy Ghost, less leeway may be allowed. (V,59)

In matters of worship, whatever Scripture clearly sets forth has first priority both as to authority and required obedience. In second place is the force of human reason and whatever it may determine. Next, whatever the Church, by her ecclesiastical authority and in harmony with reason, thinks and defines as true and good will overrule all other lesser judgments. (V,8)

Do we suppose that the Sacred Word of God can be properly honored by those who incite open contempt for the holy ordinances of the Church? No! It is not possible that such ministers can observe, as they should, the one when they are unnecessarily withdrawing their brethren from obedience to the other. (V,8)

—— *Sin (Sinners)* ——

There are in sin these three things: the act which passes away and vanishes; the pollution with which it leaves the soul defiled; and the punishment to which those who have committed it are made subject. (VI,6)

Without knowledge and awareness of sin, there can be no repentance. (Discourse on Justification)

If God should say to us…that if He searched all the generations since the fall of Adam and found only one person who had done even one act that marked him as pure, without stain or blemish of any kind, then such a person could serve as a ransom from suffering for all of us and all the angels, do you think that this single human ransom could be found among mortals? (Discourse on Justification)

No one expects to harvest grapes from thistles. Nor from a sinful nature can suitable fruits be expected. (Sermon on Pride)

Because we are weak, we all do the wrong things in many circumstances. Our virtue is that we desire to do nothing wrong. Testimony to that virtue is our prayer that we may be strengthened from above to withstand whatever sin presents itself to us. Those who pray to have sin pardoned and have not also prayed to have it prevented do so in vain. This includes praying to prevent **all** sins when we cannot name a particular transgression for which we seek pardon. (V,48)

We are lovers of pleasure more than lovers of God. Our assent to His saving truth is often withheld, not because the truth is too weak to persuade us but because the stream of corruption within us carries it away. For the mind to abide in the light of faith there must be in our will a constant resolution to have no fellowship at all with the vanities and works of darkness. (V,63)

What God usually has to say about the wicked- -whom He hates--is that they are bloodthirsty and deceitful, will not live out half their days, and that He will cause pestilence to come upon them and strike them with consuming sorrows, fevers, burning diseases, and sores that cannot be cured. The sins of the ungodly shall rob them of any peace. (V,76)

If people think that injustice and peace, sin and prosperity, can dwell together, they err. They fail to distinguish properly between a thing and that which gives it the form of happiness, between possession and fruition, between the having and the enjoying of good things. The impious cannot enjoy what they have, partly because they do not see their possessions as coming from the hands of God, who alone can make temporal blessings comfortable for us to enjoy, and partly because they place things above what is of far greater price and worth. In so doing, they turn what might have been food into poison and make their property into their own snare. Within the nest of their greatest prosperity they foolishly lay those eggs out of which their woeful overthrow will later be hatched. (V,76)

In other people's offences we see the clear image of our own weaknesses. (V,77)

—— *Social Contract (Consent)* ——

We are not by ourselves sufficient to furnish ourselves with an adequate store of things necessary for such a life as our nature desires, a life fit for the dignity of a human person. Therefore, to supply these defects and imperfections that we have living alone, we are naturally induced to seek communion and fellowship with others. This was the reason why people first united in public societies. These societies could not be without government, nor government without a distinct kind of law.… There are two foundations that support public societies, the one a natural inclination whereby all people desire social life and fellowship, the other an order expressly or secretly agreed upon concerning the manner of their union in living together. (I,10)

There was no way for people to take away all mutual grievances, injuries, and wrongs except by a composition and agreement among themselves, by ordaining some kind of public government. People made themselves subject to those whom they granted authority to rule and govern so that, through them, the peace, tranquility, and happy estate of the rest might be procured. People always knew…that strife and troubles would be endless unless they gave their common consent that all be ordered by some whom they should agree upon. Without such consent, there was no reason why one should take it upon himself or herself to be lord or judge over another. (I,10)

The lawful power of making laws to command whole political societies of people resides so properly in the society itself that, if any prince or potentate of any kind whatsoever on earth exercises such power without having expressly received his commission directly or immediately from God, or else derived it at the first from the consent of those persons upon whom he imposes laws, it is no better than mere tyranny. (I,10)

Only those are laws which public approbation has made so. But approbation is given not only by those who personally declare their assent by voice, sign, or act, but also when others do it in their behalf by right originally derived from them. So in parliaments, councils, and the similar assemblies, even though we are not personally present ourselves, our assent in such cases is given through agents acting on our behalf. And there is no reason why what we do through others should not stand as our deed, no less effectually binding us than if we ourselves had done it in person.…(I,10)

We consent to be commanded when that society of which we are a part has at any time before consented, without having revoked the same by a similar universal agreement. Therefore, just as any person's past deed is good as long as he himself continues, so the act of a public society of people agreed upon five hundred years ago stands as theirs who are presently members of those same societies. For corporations are immortal; we were then alive in our predecessors, and they still live in their successors. (I,10)

It seems to me almost beyond doubt and controversy that every independent multitude, before any certain form of government has been established, has, under God's supreme authority, full dominion over itself, just as a person not tied by a bond of subjection to another has the same kind of power over himself. God, in creating humankind, endued it naturally with the full power to guide itself with regard to what kinds of societies it would choose to live in. (VIII,3)

A person who is born lord of himself may be made another's servant, and that power which whole societies naturally have may be given to few or to one under whom the rest shall then live in subjection. (VIII,3)

It is one thing to ordain a power and another thing to bestow that power upon someone else after it has been ordained, that is, to appoint the particular holder of that power or the person in whom that power shall rest. Nature has ordained that there should be a power in civil societies to make laws. But the consent of the people (who are that society) has designated that the Prince's person will be the place where the supremacy of that power shall reside. The act of instituting such power may and sometimes does precede the act of conferring or bestowing it. And there are two different orderly ways of bestowing this power, namely, either by appointing some certain individuals--one or many--or else, without designating any person, specifying some fixed conditions concerning the quality of the persons who are to receive the power and the form or manner of their taking it. (VIII,6)

—— *Stewardship (Charitable Giving)* ——

Although nature requires that God be honored with our wealth, we, for the most part, honor wealth as though it were God. (V,79)

If we give some small portion of our wealth to charitable purposes, we think the whole duty we owe to God is fully satisfied. (V,79)

We may boldly set it down as a principle clear in nature, as an axiom not to be called into question, as an obvious and infallible truth, that we are eternally bound to honor God with our substance as a token of our thankful acknowledgement of all that we have received from Him. To honor Him with our worldly goods, not only by spending them in a lawful manner and using them without offence, but also by setting aside a reasonable portion to offer up to God as a sign that we gladly confess His sole and sovereign dominion over all, is a duty that all people are obligated to perform. (V,79)

Giving is also a part of the very worship that is required by the law of God and to which all people are no less strictly bound than to any other natural duty. (V,79)

Generous and liberal contributions are required of those who prosper, partly as a sign of their own joy at God's goodness to them and partly as a means to help the poor and needy. (V,70)

Whatever in nature excels in pre-eminence and honor is of greatest value and benefit to other things. This fact should be an inducement to God's children to delight in imparting to others the good that has been bestowed upon them in proportion to what they have received. The good things in life are known to be communicable by those who possess them; they are known to be derived from others and to be transferable to those in need of them. (Sermon on Pride/Justice)

Since the greatest among those whom we honor are those to whom we bring the most valuable and carefully chosen presents, it follows that if we dare not disgrace our worldly superiors by offering the sort of refuse that we bring to God Himself, we are showing clearly that our acknowledgment of God's greatness is only a pretence. In our hearts we love and fear God less than we dread the great men among us. (V,34)

Our hearts cling to earthly things, admire them for the power they produce in this world, and usually credit their possession either to nature or to chance and fortune. We think little about the grace and providence from which they actually came. Unless by some kind of regular tribute we acknowledge God's dominion, it may not be doubted that in a short time we will learn to forget whose tenants we are and suppose that the world is our own absolute, free, and independent inheritance. (V,79)

We know that God Himself has no need of worldly goods. He takes them because it is good for us that He do so. (V,79)

Whether we give to God that which He has commanded of us, or that which a vote of the Church thinks we should allot from our resources, or what our own private devotions lead us to give, we should remember that our gift is not only a testimony of our affection for God but also a means to maintain our religion, which cannot endure without the help of such temporal support. (V,79)

Even as the life of the clergyman is spent in God's service, so he is sustained by revenue that is given to God. It is therefore proper to call payments to the minister a token of the oblation we offer to God. (V,74)

— *Superstition* —

Superstition does not know the right kind or observe the proper measure of actions that are appropriate to the worship of God. Rather, superstition is always linked with a false view of divinity. Whether from excessive enthusiasm or fear, superstition produces an erroneous relationship with God, teaching us neither what we should abhor nor what we should worship. (V,3)

Superstition may elevate the true God but defrauds Him by producing needless observances or bestowing honors on others that belong to Him. This leads either to idolatry or a needless superfluity of religious creeds and practices. (V,3)

— *Thanksgivings* —

There is good reason why we should delight more in giving thanks to God than in making requests. Asking is filled with pensiveness and fear; thanksgiving always has joy attached to it. The one belongs to those who seek; the other to those who have found happiness. Those who pray for something only sow; those who give thanks declare what they have reaped. (V,43)

— *Theology* —

What is the whole drift of the Scripture of God but to teach theology? What is theology but the science of things divine? What science can be attained without the help of natural discourse and reason? (III,8)

Scripture indeed teaches things beyond nature, things which our reason by itself could not reach. Yet we also believe these things because reason tells us that the Scripture is the Word of God. (III,8)

Because we maintain that in Scripture we are taught all things necessary for salvation, it is very childishly demanded by some to know what Scripture there is that can teach us that the Scripture is the sacred authority upon which knowledge of our whole faith and salvation depends. As though there were any kind of science in the world that leads people into knowledge without presupposing a number of things already known. No science makes known the first principles upon which it builds. Rather, these principles are always taken as either plain and manifest in themselves or as proved and granted already, some former knowledge having made them evident. (III,8)

— *Time (And Motion)* —

As nature brought forth time with motion, we have learned by observing motion how to divide time and, by smaller units of time, how to measure its larger units as well as how to measure how long everything else will last. Time itself is nothing but the force and flux of that very instant when the motion of the heavens began. When applied to other things, time is the length of their continuation as measured by the distance between the instant of their beginning and the present instant, just as the time of a person's life is his continuance from the instant of his birth until the instant of his last gasp. (V,69)

The motion by which we measure time is circular and the compass of that circuit is such that the heavens are continually moving within it, keeping those motions at uniform speed so that they repeatedly touch the same points. In so doing they cannot help but bring us back frequently to the same distances and times. Time is nothing but the quantity of that continuance that all things have that are not, like God, without a beginning. (V,69)

Time only measures. It does not have any effect on what it measures or on itself. When we say that "time eats," or "sorts out all things," or "is the wisest thing in the world" because of what it brings forth, or that "nothing is more foolish than time," because it never holds anything for long or because whatever it learns one day it forgets the next, or that days are prosperous for some people and miserable for others--all of these sayings *about* time are not true of time itself. These are all characteristics of other things that are in time and, because of a close association with time, either lay their burdens on her back or their crowns on her head. Yes, the very opportunities that we ascribe to time actually adhere to the things with which time is joined. As for time, it neither causes things nor the possibility of things, though it consists of both. (V,69)

Everything has its time. The works of God have a time that is most seasonable and suitable for them. Some of His works are ordinary and some special but all are worthy of observation. (V,69)

There is no doubt that, just as God's extraordinary presence has hallowed and sanctified certain places, so His extraordinary works, which have truly and worthily advanced certain times, ought to lead all people who honor God to regard those dates as holier than others. (V,69)

— *Tithing* —

In receiving a little, God blesses all. (V,79)

Those who hold back the tithe payment do not harm God but they wrong Him by doing so. Thinking that they are relieving themselves of a debt, they are actually wounding themselves, unless they believe that God deluded the world when he said, "Bring all your tithes into the storehouse that there may be meat in my house." (V,79)

In addition to other rare donations of unpredictable amounts and regularity, there is good reason why one-tenth of ones income came to be regarded as appropriate revenue to be allotted to God. Are not all things created by God is such a way that the forms that give them their distinction are *number*, their operations, *measure*, their matter, *weight*? *Three* is the mystical number of God's unfathomable perfection within Himself; *seven* is the number whereby our own perfections are most ordered, through grace; *ten* is the number of nature's perfections because the beauty of nature is order, and the foundation of order is number, and ten is the highest number we can reach without repeating the numbers under it. Could nature better acknowledge the power of God in nature than by assigning Him that quantity that contains all that she possesses? (V,79)

When the properties that we tithe had seemed to be our own, we had liberty to use them as we thought best. But once we made them His--which they always were--we should have been warned by the example of others about what happens when we try to clip the coin that has the mark of God on it. (V,79)

The most honest and safe way for God always to have the tithe that is due Him is by making payments to Him in kind, out of the riches that the earth continuously yields from His gracious benediction. We know that what comes to us from God, in the natural course of His providence, is innocent and pure and, perhaps, most acceptable, because it is less spotted with the stain of unlawful or indirect procurement. Besides, whereas prices change every day, nature, which is constant, is always the fairest and most permanent standard between God and us. (V,79)

By means of the tithe the lowest and the very poorest of people give to God as much in proportion to their income as the richest--and, in affection, many times more. In this way, the poor always have the tithe as a real token to assure themselves that in God's sight they are equals in acceptance, protection, divine privileges, and all pre-eminences--equals and peers of those to whom they are inferiors in earthly matters. (V,79)

—— *Toleration* ——

No one can tell, of course, who is a true believer and who is, inwardly, an unbeliever; no one can tell except God whose eyes alone behold the secret dispositions of all men's hearts. We whose eyes are too dim to behold the inner person must leave the judgment of each other to the Lord, taking everyone as he presents himself and counting all as brothers and sisters, assuming that Christ loves them tenderly so long as they continue to profess the Gospel and to join outwardly in the communion of saints. (First Sermon on Jude)

Such is the perverse constitution of our nature that we neither understand perfectly the way of the Lord, nor steadfastly embrace it when it is understood, nor graciously utter it when it is embraced, nor peaceably maintain it when it is preached. The best of us is overtaken sometimes by blindness, sometimes by impatience, sometimes by other passions of the mind to which, as God knows, we are subject. We must, therefore, be content to pardon others and crave their pardon in all such matters. Let no one think himself free from mistakes or oversights in his speech. (Discourse on Justification)

God has not given us any clear way to comprehend-- and thus no permission to seek out--which particular persons are certain heirs of His kingdom and which are castaways. However, we may, until the end of the world, always assume that, in so far as we have the power to discern what other people are, and in so far as we have any duty to ascertain their relation with God, the safest axiom of charity for us to rest upon is that whoever says he believes is a child of God, and whoever says he does not is not. (V,49)

It is not proper for us, in this life, to condemn anyone because for all we know there is hope that everyone who repents before his death will be forgiven. Charity, which hopes for all things, also prays for all people. We must stop pretending to have a personal knowledge of who is a vessel of wrath and who of mercy. We have not the capacity to know who others really are in the sight of God. For us there is sufficient evidence in the condition of all people to justify our prayer to God in their behalf. (V,49)

God does not require us to dive into other people's consciences. Nor does their fraud and deceit hurt anyone but themselves. To God they seem to be what they are but we must take them as they seem to be. In God's eyes those who are not truly and sincerely with Christ are against Him. In our eyes, those who make no outward show against Christ must be received as being with Him. (V,68)

— *Tradition (Custom, Experience)* —

Let novelty give way and let ancient custom prevail. (V,39)

It is rightly said that gray hair denotes ripeness of understanding and that old age denotes virtue. (V,7)

Wisdom and youth are rarely combined in one person. (V,7)

Those in whom time has not yet perfected knowledge must be content to follow those in whom it has. (V,7)

Sharp and subtle discourses often procure very great applause but they are outweighed in the balance by that which custom and experience have clearly shown us.

When we compare authorities, person for person, in order to decide to whom we will listen, we find the aged, for the most part, the best experienced and the least subject to rash and ill-advised passions. (V,7)

It is the voice of both God and nature, not only of human learning, that tells us that in matters of policy and actions the sentences and judgments of men who are experienced, aged and wise are to be listened to even if they speak without proof or demonstration, for they are themselves the demonstration of the truth of what they say. (V,7)

I mean by tradition those ordinances made in the earliest days of the Christian religion, established with the authority that Christ has bestowed on His Church in matters indifferent [not essential to salvation] and required to be observed until the Church finds just and reasonable reasons to change them. (V,65)

The world does not tolerate the idea that we are wiser than all those who have gone before us. (V,7)

There is good reason why we should be slow to change the ancient and long-approved religious customs and rites of our venerable predecessors unless there is some very urgent necessity to do so. The love of old things argues for their conservation, whereas shallowness and lack of experience will probably lead only to innovation for its own sake even before the new thing is tried. (V,7)

Surely the fact that antiquity, custom, and the consensual usage in the Church all conform to what present church law ordains is sufficient reason to continue these religious observances, unless some significant inconvenience requires the contrary. (V,7)

Everything that is expedient and necessary for the ordering of spiritual matters cannot, of course, be of ancient provenance. The Church, as a body that never dies, always has as much power to ordain what never has been practiced in the past as it does to ratify what has gone before. (V,8)

Sometimes it happens that a thing that is no longer necessary for the purpose for which it was intended--or to which is might be applied--may nevertheless be retained even though it is not used, lest the removal of it might cause damage to something to which it necessarily adheres. For this reason, those who have lost all possibility of sight keep their eyes where nature put them. (V,42)

Insofar as possible, nature always inclines toward validation and preservation. Dissolutions and eliminations of what has been done in the past are not only to be opposed but also to be hated when urged without good cause or beyond what is reasonable. (V,62)

Lest the name of tradition should be offensive to anyone, considering how far it has been and is abused by some, we mean by traditions those ordinances made in the prime of Christian religion, established with that authority which Christ left to the Church for matters indifferent, and therefore requisite to be observed until similar authority find just and reasonable cause to alter them. So ecclesiastical traditions are not to be rudely or grossly shaken off just because the inventors of them were human. (V,65)

Those who add all religious traditions to supernatural and necessary truth...are in error. ... We reject such ideas not only because they are not in Scripture, but also because they cannot otherwise be sufficiently demonstrated by reason to be proved to come from God. Traditions that are from God, and may be clearly proved to be so, we do not deny to be the truth, even though they are unwritten. Nor do we deny that they have the same force and authority as the written laws of God. (I,14)

Those rites and customs known to be Apostolic and, having the nature of things changeable, were dealt with by the Church in the same way as other things of that kind, that is, they were regarded as subject to change, even though they were not set down in the Apostles' writings. For both the written and the unwritten, being known to be Apostolic, it is not the manner of delivery to the Church, but the author from whom they proceed that gives them their force and credit. (I,14)

We should not rudely and grossly shake off ecclesiastical traditions simply because men invented them. (V,65)

Our lives in this world are guided partly by rules and partly by examples. To draw our duties in each particular situation from discourse on general rules and axioms is both troublesome and often so full of difficulty that is makes deliberations hard and tedious even for the wisest person. Instead, we are inclined to look for examples to show what others have done before us. It is easier for us to follow such patterns than to enter into new deliberations especially if, because of their wisdom and virtue, we think that those whose examples we follow have proceeded without error. (V,65)

— *Trinity* —

Our God is one, or rather, Oneness itself, a complete unity, having nothing but Itself in Itself, and not consisting (as do all things besides God) of many things. Nevertheless, in this essential unity of God a personal Trinity exists in a manner far exceeding the possibility of human conceptualization. The outward works of God are of such a kind that, even in His oneness, each Person that is Him has in Him something special and unique to Itself. For being three, all subsist in the essence of one Deity: all things are from the Father, by the Son, through the Spirit. That which the Son hears from the Father and which the Spirit receives from the Father and the Son, the same we have at the hands of the Spirit as being the last, and therefore the nearest to us in order, although in power the same with the second and the first. (I,2)

If we respect God's glory in itself, that glory is the equal right and possession of all three Persons of the Godhead, without any superiority or difference among them. (V,42)

Seeing That the Father comes from no other source and the Son is from the Father and the Spirit from both, they are each, by their several properties, distinguishable from one another. The Father is identified by the property of being from no other, the Son by the property of being from the Father, and the Holy Ghost by the property of being from the Father and the Son. Thus there is in each **Person** implied both the substance of God, which is one, and that other characteristic that causes each to be really and truly different from the other two. Each has its own nature, which neither of the other has; but each also has the same nature. For example, no one but Peter can be the **person** that Peter is yet Paul has the same **nature** as Peter. (V,51)

The persons of the Godhead, because of the unity of their substance, necessarily remain within one another, just as surely as they are distinguished from one another. Two of them are the offspring of one and one is the offspring of the other two. Since all three are but one God, indivisible in essence and substance, their distinction is not a separation. (V,56)

Whatever God does, the hands of all three Persons of the Godhead are jointly and equally involved, each according to the order of the connection that makes Him dependent upon the others. Although, in this sense, the Father is first, the Son second, and the Spirit last--and consequently closest to the effects of every deed done by all three--they are all of one essence and one effect. (V,56)

The Father as goodness, the Son as Wisdom, the Holy Ghost as power all concur in every particular aspect as they issue from that one glorious Deity, which they all are. That which motivates God is goodness. That which orders His work is wisdom. That which perfects His work is power. (V,56)

— *Truth* —

There are but two ways whereby the Spirit leads people to all truth: the one extraordinary, the other common. The first is given only to a few, the other extends itself to all who are God's. The one we call, in an especially divine and excellent way, "revelation," the other, "reason." (Pref. 3.10)

— *Union With God* —

Nothing may be infinitely desired except that good which is indeed infinite. What is better is more desirable; what is most desirable is that in which there is an infinity of goodness, so that if any thing is infinitely desirable it must be the highest of all things that are desired. No good is infinite except God alone; therefore He alone is our felicity and bliss. Moreover, desire tends toward union with that which it desires. If then in Him we are blessed, it is by the power of our participation and conjunction with Him. Again, it is not the possession of any good thing that can make those happy who have it, unless they enjoy the thing with which they are possessed. Therefore, we are happy when we fully enjoy God as an object wherein the powers of our souls are satisfied even with everlasting delight. So even though we are human, yet by being united to God we live, as it were, the life of God. (I,11)

Complete union with God must encompass every power and faculty of our minds that is able to receive so glorious an object. We are capable of God both by understanding and will. We are capable of God by understanding because He is that sovereign truth which comprehends the rich treasures of all wisdom; by will because He is that sea of goodness which forever satisfies the thirst of whomever tastes of it. (I,11)

As the will now seeks God by desiring Him, which is, as it were, a motion towards an end not yet obtained, so likewise after the end has been attained the will works by love. … Whereas we now love the thing that is good--but good especially in respect of our own benefit--we shall then love the thing that is good only or principally for the beauty of goodness in itself. Insofar as the soul is active, it will be perfected by love of that infinite good; insofar as it is passive, it will also be perfected with those supernatural passions of joy, peace, and delight, all of which will be endless and everlasting. (I,11)

— *Vestments* —

We believe that our vestments suit well the joyful spirit with which God is delighted when His saints praise Him. They also help ministers resemble the glory of the saints in heaven, as well as the beauty with which angels have appeared on earth. (V,29)

There is not one sentence in all of God's Scripture that disallows the wearing of vestments in the manner and for the purpose required by the Church of England. (V,29)

What clerical habit or attire is most suitable for each order of ministry to use in the course of its everyday work in order to indicate both the seriousness of the position and to provide an example to others, is something too frivolous to be argued about. (V,78)

The attire that the minister of God is authorized to wear during divine worship is only a matter of good form, something that has been judged by our leaders to be appropriate and in harmony with the outward symbolic tokens of the various actions in the service or the status of those performing them. (V,29)

We wear this attire not because we think ourselves holier by doing so. Neither should those who do not follow this practice think us unholy for doing so. (V,29)

The wearing of vestments is only an indifferent matter authorized because in our laws the wisdom of our church has deemed it appropriate to do so. (V,29)

If a bishop, priest, deacon, and the rest of the ecclesiastical order come forward to administer the usual sacrifice in a white garment, are they thereby God's adversaries? Clerks, monks, widows, virgins, take heed! It is dangerous for you to be seen otherwise than in dirty and ragged clothes--to say nothing of secular men who are proclaimed to be at war with God whenever they put on expensive or ostentatious clothes. (V,29)

Is it not better that the love which we bear God should make the little things that we employ in His service comfortable rather than that by an overly scrupulous dislike of so small a thing as vestments we withdraw our hearts and affections from the worship of God? (V,29)

All well-ordered polities [including churches] have always judged it proper to distinguish each class of person from each other class, when they are in public, by certain adornments. In this way everyone may receive such respect and honor as is due his status and profession even if he is not known personally. Anyone who finds fault with these appropriate distinctions must have an unbalanced mind. (V,78)

— *Virtue And Vice* —

Virtue is always clearly recognized. Its rareness causes it to be noticed and its goodness to be honored with admiration. As for iniquity and sin, they are often hidden. (V,76)

Vices have not only virtues but other vices as opposites. It may be dangerous to seek out only that which is contrary to our present evils. In maladies and sicknesses of the mind we cannot always measure good only by its distance from evil. One vice may, in some respect, be more opposite to another than either of them is from that virtue that stands between them. Liberality and covetousness, the one a virtue and the other a vice, are not so contrary to one another as the vices of covetousness and prodigality. Religion and superstition have more in common, though one is light and the other darkness, than superstition and blasphemy, which are both horrible extremes. (V,65)

Our very virtues may be snares to entrap us. The enemy that waits for any occasion to work our ruin has always found it harder to overthrow a humble sinner than a proud saint. There is no one's position so dangerous as his whom Satan has persuaded that his own righteousness shall present him pure and blameless in the sight of God. (Discourse on Justification)

Among earthly blessings, wealth is the least important and reputation the most important. For this reason we regard the gain of honor as worth the loss of all worldly benefits. Honor is commonly presumed to be a sign of more than ordinary virtue and merit, so much so that ambitious people thirst after it. (V,76)

Because there is no guarantee of the continuation of all this worldly goodness, nature has taught us to value such things not for their own sake but with reference and relation to what is independently good, namely, the exercise of virtue and the contemplation of truth. No one whose desires are rightly ordered would wish to live, breathe, and move without performing those deeds that are becoming to a person of excellent character. (V,76)

If a fair survey were made, we would discover that those who are correctly reputed to be good people are those whose virtues are many and faults tolerable. Such people we may regard as fortunate so long as their prosperity and happiness flourish in such a way that they are not a spectacle that brings misery to others. (V,76)

— *Wealth* —

Given our corrupt inclination to abuse the blessing of almighty God, prosperity usually proves to be dangerous for the souls of men. Wealth is death to the wicked and prosperity slays the foolish. Their table is a snare and their felicity is their utter ruin. There are few people who are prosperous for long and do not sin. (V,48)

What wise person ever thought fools happy? If the wicked were wise they would cease to be wicked. Their iniquity proving their folly, how can we doubt their misery? They abound in those things that all people desire. But it is a poor happiness to possess such things. A person to whom God has given riches and treasures may lack nothing that he desires; yet God has not given him the power to enjoy what he has. Solomon says that such prosperity is but vanity, something of no value. (Sermon on Remedy Against Sorrow and Fear)

— *Wisdom* —

Wisdom professes to teach human beings, and to teach them every good way: but not every good way by one way of teaching. Whatever humans on earth or angels in heaven know, it is as a drop of that unending fountain of wisdom, the treasures of which have been diversely imparted to the world. As her ways are of different kinds, so her manner of teaching is not always one and the same. Some things wisdom reveals by the sacred books of Scripture; some things by the glorious works of nature; some things she inspires from above by spiritual influence; in some things she leads and trains only by worldly experience and practice. We should not so admire any one kind of knowledge that we disgrace any other, but let all the ways of wisdom be adored according to their place and degree. (II,1)

—— *Women (Childbirth)* ——

The fruit of marriage is birth. The companion of birth is labor, the pain of which is extreme and the danger great. Dare we open our mouths to censure the Church for allowing women to show publicly their thankfulness to God for delivering them from child birth. (V,74)

It is nothing but an overflowing of gall to interpret a woman's absence from Church during the time of her pregnancy in such a way as to judge her unholy and excluded from God's House according to some ancient Levitical law. (V,74)

These most learned Divines who scoff at a pregnant woman's attire, which all that could be devised as decent during such a difficult time in her life, or make a joke out of something they are loath to show their faces for, only shows that they are more frivolous than wise. As for the women themselves, God accepts the service that they faithfully offer to Him even if they must suffer sarcastic men who mix their religious zeal with scorn for women. (V,74)

— *Works* —

The best things we do have something in them that requires God's pardon. So how can we do anything truly meritorious and worthy of reward? God freely promises a blessed life to all who sincerely keep His law even if they cannot do so perfectly. So we acknowledge the duty to do our best but renounce any claim that we thereby earn God's grace. God knows that our little *fruit of holiness* is corrupt and unsound. We are to put no confidence in it. We are to challenge nothing in the world because of it. We dare not call God to recognize our works as if we held Him in our debt. Rather our continual prayer to Him is, and must be, to bear our infirmities and pardon our offences. (Discourse on Justification)

That God rewards His servants comes not from the worthiness of our deeds but from His goodness. By the rich and unspeakable wisdom of His providence, the world and everything in it is given to us so that as we serve God so will all other things serve Him, each in their own degree and order. (Sermon on Proverbs/ Matthew/Hebrews)

To trust in works without prayer signifies impiety and blasphemy. (Sermon on Matthew 7.7)

It is repugnant to say that we are saved by the worthiness of our actions. In so saying we deny the grace of our Lord Jesus Christ. We debase, annul, and annihilate the benefit of His bitter passion if we rest in the proud imagination that life everlasting is deservedly ours, that we merit it, that we are worthy of it. (Discourse on Justification)

Works are an addition to the foundation of our faith. So be it. What of that? Surely faith is not subverted by every addition to it. Simply to add to fundamental faith in Christ is not necessarily to mingle wine with dirty water, heaven with earth, things polluted with Christ's sanctified blood. (Discourse on justification)

Our vocation is to listen to the Gospel, express the fruits, or works, of the Spirit, and persevere in hope, faith, and holy living. (Discourse on Justification)

— *Worldview* — *(Order And Interdependence)*

God created nothing simply for itself. Each thing has such an interest in all things and each part in every part so that in the whole world nothing is found wherein one part can say, "I don't need you." (Sermon on Pride/Justice)

Our Lord, the supreme commander, arranged it so that each creature should have some particular task and charge that goes beyond its own preservation. The sun does us good by giving us heat and light, the moon and stars by their secret influences, the air and wind by every one of their many qualities, the earth by receiving all of these and transmitting them to her inhabitants. How beneficial by their very nature are the operations of all things. We are unable to grasp fully the extent of these benefits in part because of God's incomprehensible greatness and in part because of our own inattention and carelessness. (Sermon on Pride/Justice)

What if nature should violate her course and cease altogether (though it were but for a brief time) to observe her own laws? What if those principal and mother elements whereof all things in this lower world are made should lose the qualities they now have and the frame of that heavenly arch erected over our heads should loosen and dissolve itself? What if the celestial spheres should forget their accustomed motions and by irregular volubility turn themselves any way they wished? What if the prince of the lights of heaven (who now as a giant runs his unwearied course) should, as it were, through a languishing faintness begin to stand and rest himself? What if the moon should wander from her beaten way or the times and seasons of the year blend themselves by disordered and confused mixture, or the winds breathe out their last gasp, the clouds yield no rain, or the earth be denied any heavenly influence, or the fruits of the earth pine away as children at the withered breasts of their mother no longer able to give them relief, what would become of man himself, whom all these things do now serve? (I,3)

There is no living in a public society without order, because the lack of order is the mother of confusion. Without order, division necessarily follows, and out of division inevitable destruction. Therefore, the Apostle [Paul], giving instructions to public societies, requires that all things be done in order (1 Cor. 14:40). There can be no order among things unless there is a settlement among the individuals involved concerning the persons who are authorized to be conversant about them. And if things or persons are ordered, this implies that they are distinguished by degrees. For order is a gradual disposition. The whole world consists of so many and different kinds of parts that it is only upheld by this order. God, who created them has set them in a certain order. Yes, the very Deity Himself both keeps and forever requires the following to be kept as a law: that wherever there is a coalition of many, the lowest is to be knit to the highest by that which, being nearest to it will cause each to cleave to the other and so all to continue as one. (VIII,2)

Worship (Corporate)

The outer performance of our worship, which is visible, should represent what our inner affection to God, which is invisible, ought to be. (V,6)

It is generally agreed that the importance and dignity of any sort of behavior is measured by the worth of the subject performing the acts and the worth of the object toward which they are directed. In both respects we must acknowledge that our world affords nothing comparable to public corporate worship. (V,6)

Since man is the worthiest creature on earth, and since every community of people is worthier than any single person in it, and since the most excellent community is the one we call the Church, then there can be no work in the world equal to the exercise of corporate public worship which is the proper operation of the Church of God. (V,6)

Religious rites performed by whole societies should have in them, so far as it can be achieved, an excellence corresponding to the majesty of Him whom we worship. (V,6)

We should not lightly esteem what has been sanctioned as a suitable form of worship by the judgment of the ancient Church or the continuous practice of the Church through history. Experience shows that it is not safe to swerve unnecessarily from these precedents. (V,7)

The first thing that should, with a clear conscience, yield approval of established worship practices is not so much that a good examination shows them in all cases to be superior to any others that might possibly be devised--for whoever required such a standard from any human rule--but only that they are convenient and suitable for the purposes they are designed to serve. (V,4)

Laws concerning worship are changeable by the authority of the Church; articles concerning doctrine are not. (V,8)

In matters of worship, whatever Scripture clearly sets forth has first priority both as to authority and required obedience. In second place is the force of human reason and whatever it may determine. Next, whatever the Church, by her ecclesiastical authority and in harmony with reason, thinks and defines as true and good will overrule all other lesser judgments. (V,8)

The simple consensus of the Church in matters of worship should, in itself, shut the mouths of those who live inside the Church and yet dare to bark at her. (V,8)

Even as the overall form of our corporate worship is not a matter of individual preference, neither should the parts of the service be left to voluntary choice. Rather, these are all set down in that order and manner that the Church, in its wisdom has thought best-suited both for special occasions and for the general objective of glorifying God. (V,19)

— *Zeal* —

If the minister does not praise God with all his energy, if he fails to exert his soul in prayer, if he does take to heart the needs of his people and speak out as Moses, Daniel and Ezra did for their people, then how can there be anything but frozen coldness in those whose hearts should be set on fire but who see their leader's affections benumbed? (V,25)

It is dangerous when in religious matters we tend too much toward either zeal or fear. (V,3)

Zeal, unless it is constrained when is strives against either what is or what it imagines to be even remotely contrary to religion, uses its cutting edge with such eagerness that the existence of religion itself is threatened. Through excessive hatred of the weeds, the corn in God's field is ripped out. (V,3)

Religious zeal, unless properly limited, will lead a person to be so eager to please God that he will do what does not please Him at all. (V,3)

When we compare those who swerve too far in the direction of excessive enthusiasm with the sincere, sound and discreet faith of Abraham, their actions seem like flattery and his like the faithful service of friendship. (V,3)

ABOUT THE AUTHORS

—— *Philip Secor* ——

Philip Secor is a leading authority on the life and thought of Richard Hooker. His acclaimed biography, *Richard Hooker Prophet of Anglicanism* (Burns & Oates/Anglican Book Centre, 1999) and his two modern editions of Hooker's most important writings, *The Sermons of Richard Hooker* (SPCK, 2001) and *Richard Hooker on Anglican Faith and Worship* (SPCK, 2003) have made Hooker's life and thought widely available in the English speaking world.

Secor holds his BA from Drew University and his MA and PhD from Duke University. He has taught at Duke, Dickinson College and Davidson College and been Dean of the College at Muhlenberg College and President of Cornell College. He lives with his wife, Anne, in eastern Pennsylvania.

—— *Lee W. Gibbs* ——

Lee W. Gibbs is a widely recognized religious scholar in the Episcopal Church. He is one of the co-editors of the authoritative *Folger Library Edition of the Works of Richard Hooker* (1977-1998) and the author of many articles on Hooker in such publications as *Harvard Theological Review*.

Gibbs is an Episcopal priest in the Diocese of Ohio and had been a professor of religious studies at Case Western Reserve University and Cleveland State University. He holds his BA from Macalester College and his STB and ThD from Harvard. He lives with his wife, Joan, in eastern Ohio.

Made in the USA
Columbia, SC
20 December 2019

85558346R00120